I0471742

بسم الله الرحمن الرحيم

In The Name Of God The Most Gracious The Most Merciful

بسم الله الرحمن الرحيم

In The Name Of God The Most Gracious The Most Merciful

H.R.H Prince Saud Alhassan Saud
Abdulaziz Al Saud

5/16/2012

This book explains the Islamic law that applies the Quran and Sunnah as a constitution, and the concept of Rahma. It will emphasize this concept by explaining the rigid law of Hudod, then elaborating on Rahma.

Copyright © 2012, H.R.H Prince Saud Alhassan Saud Abdulaziz Al Saud

All rights reserved. No part of this book may be reproduced, stored, or transmitted by any means—whether auditory, graphic, mechanical, or electronic—without written permission of both publisher and author, except in the case of brief excerpts used in critical articles and reviews. Unauthorized reproduction of any part of this work is illegal and is punishable by law.

Hardback ISBN 978-1-105-95768-0
Paperback ISBN 978-1-105-90427-1

بسم الله الرحمن الرحيم

عن عبدالله بن عمرو، وأبي هريرة رضي اللّه عنهما قالا: قال رسول اللّه صلى الله عليه وسلم: ‟إذا حكَمَ الحاكم، فاجتهد وأصاب، فلَه أجران. وإذا حكَمَ، فاجتهد فأخطأ، فله أجر واحد‟ متفق عليه. *أخرجه: البخاري في ‟صحيحه‟ رقم: 7352, ومسلم في‟صحيحه‟ رقم: 1716*

المراد بالحاكم: هو الذي عنده من العلم ما يؤهله للقضاء. وقد ذكر أهل العلم شروط القاضي. فبعضهم بالغ فيها، وبعضهم اقتصر على العلم الذي يصلح به للفتوى

إن هذا العمل إجتهاد يحتمل الصواب و الخطأ، فأرجوا تصحيحي إن أخطأت

أشكر الله سبحانه و تعالى و أحمده على اتمامي هذا البحث.

أهدي هذا العمل المتواضع إلي من هدى بالجواب الصحيح حيرة سائليه فأظهر بسماحته تواضع العلماء وبرحابته سماحة العارفين، سيدي صاحب السمو الملكي الأمير/ نايف بن عبدالعزيز ولي العهد نائب رئيس مجلس الوزراء وزير الداخلية ـ حفظه الله.

ثم إلى من افتقده في مواجهة الصعاب ولم تمهله الدنيا لأرتوي من حنانه والدي صاحب السمو الملكي الأمير/ الحسن بن سعود بن عبدالعزيز، رحمه الله. وأدعوا الله أن يجعل ثواب هذا العمل في ميزان حسناته.

I thank God Almighty, and I praise Him for being able to complete this work. I dedicate this humble work to the person who guides mislead people with the correct answers, and shows by his patience and forgiveness the modesty and tolerance of the knowledgeable, my beloved uncle, Crown Prince Naif Bin Abdulaziz, Deputy Premier and Minister of Interior.

I also dedicate this book to the person I miss the most, one who was not granted much time in this world, my father, H.R.H Prince Alhassan Bin Saud Bin Abdulaziz. God rest his soul.

Contents

Introduction

Islam is the eternal religion that God revealed to his messenger, Muhammad (peace be upon him). It does not matter what negative attitude others take to this religion. It is the unquestionable faith of Muslims, and not a subject of doubt. This must not in any way intimidate or terrorize others from scientific discussions and arguments, there should not be any compulsion into Islam. "There is no compulsion in religion."[1] Islam in its essence tends to be intellectual and directed primarily to appeal to reason and logic.

As we know, Islam is the main basis of Saudi Arabia's legal system; in fact the Quran and Sunnah (the teachings and practices of Prophet Muhammad) constitute the country's constitution. The Islamic legal system has six capital crimes, which are called "Hudod" and Qisas, and requires the protection of the five necessities (religion, people's lives, their minds and intellect, honor and family, money and equity). In this thesis I will explain the application of Hudod (limits) in Islamic Law. I will demonstrate that under this rigid Law of Hudod lays a hidden and essentially important system of mercy and forgiveness in the applications of Rahma and Sitr (mercy and protect/shelter/cover).

---

[1] Quran, 2 (surat albaqara): 256.

Historical Background on Saudi Arabia and Its Legal System

Some might doubt the existence of sharia law systems, and in fact most of the sharia applying states apply it in their statutes but have a written constitution that does not constitute the Quran and Sunnah as its constitution. The Saudi legal system differs from such states; it applies a full Islamic system of governance. Saudi Arabia could be the only state that has an announced constitution of the Quran and Sunnah. The model of Sharia law and concepts of Rahma and Sitr could only be imagined in such systems. Thus it is important to explain how the Saudi system evolved and promulgated the Quran and Sunnah as its constitution.

In 1924 Abdulaziz ibn Saud, founder and first King of Saudi Arabia, took control of the western region of Hijaz. By that act he ended a long series of battles to join and unite a vast but fragmented Kingdom. King Abdulaziz had his eyes on fulfilling his goal of building a nation that would fit the aspiration and needs of the people, while growing alongside their assessment of what would best serve them and their nation. He knew that Islam provided the only means of uniting this nation, reflecting its deep importance to the culture and history of the Arabian Peninsula.[2] National unity was realized because King Abdulaziz applied the Principles of Islam to public policy and all other fields of life. He was able not only to unify the country but also able to prove the reliability of the Islamic solution and demonstrate its validity for his time and thereon after.

---

[2] *See* Ahmed H. Dahlaan, Dirasa Fi al Siyasah al Dakhiliyah Li Al Mamlakah al Arabia al Saudia [Study in the Internal Politics of the Kingdom of Saudi Arabia] 31–33 (1984); Faisal bin Mishal, Islamic Political Development in the Kingdom of Saudi Arabia; Majlis Al Shura: Concept, Theory and Practice 51 (2002).

King Abdulaziz was gradually transforming a simple administrative structure into a series of well-defined and organized institutions that administered and assisted the executive authority that managed the affairs of an expanding Kingdom. He focused on the needs of his people by establishing a system of governance that implemented Islamic based principles of consultation, as presented in the Quran (Islam's Holy Book) and Sunnah (teachings, actions, and traditions of the Prophet peace be upon him).[3] The *National Council*, (Almajlis Al Ahli) a consultative council introduced by King Abdulaziz in 1924, began to take on powers, except for the powers of foreign and military affairs that remained in the hands of the King. In August 1925 the Makkah Consultative Council was formed. The Makkah Council has greater powers; the Council was responsible for overseeing internal security, trade, education, communication, the court system, and municipal affairs. It was the center for the General Consultative council, which played a major role in the creation the Council of Ministers.

In 1926 King Abdulaziz approved a constitution that was called (Al Talimat Al Asasiyah) the Basic Regulations for the Hijaz region. The document resembled the constitutions of modern states and may also be viewed as the predecessor for future ones. The Hijaz Constitution had nine sections with a total of seventy-nine articles, which dealt with the system of government, the administrative responsibility, the Department of Accounts, the General Inspectorate, the Municipal Councils. Most importantly, the fourth article of this document established several governmental bodies, which included the Village and Tribal Councils, Administrative Councils, Consultative Council, and District Councils.[4]

King Abdulaziz formed the Commission of Inspection and Reform in 1927. The Commission was tasked to review the administrative system, and the commission sent a proposal to legislate a new statute for the Consultative Council that was

---

[3] *See* Faisal Faisal ibn Mishal, *supra*note 1, at 41 and 65; The Majlis al Shura Council Home Page, *Shura in the Kingdom of Saudi Arabia: A Historical Background, Majlis alShura*, http://www.shura.gov.sa/wps/wcm/connect/ShuraEn/internet/Historical+BG (Last Visited march 3, 2012).
[4] *See* Soliman A. Sulaim, Constitutional and Judicial Organization in Saudi Arabia 3–26 (1970) (unpublished Ph.D. dissertation, Johns Hopkins University) (in file with author); Ahmed H. Dahlan, *supra* note 1, at 121–126.

approved by the King in July 1927. The new Council had the duty to inform and report the government about errors in the application of the laws and statutes. The Council was also responsible for work in other areas that included the budget, expropriation of public property, construction project licenses, law and statute legislation, and employment of foreign nationals.[5]

In the late 1920s King Abdulaziz started to face modernity. The Arabian kingdom was faced with a modern world to compete in. Due to the complexities of modernity, King Abdulaziz sanctioned more reform recommendations from the Commission of Inspection, thus the Council of Deputies (Majlis Al Wikala) was formed in January 1932. In the twenty-three years of its functioning, The Council of Deputies served as a small council of ministers for the Hijaz region until 1953, when the Council of Ministers was created and all the provinces of the Kingdom were brought under Council of Ministers' jurisdiction.[6] On the 23rd of September 1932, the Kingdom was united as the Kingdom of Saudi Arabia. This brought all the Saudi citizens under a unified constitutional and administrative system, while allowing the completion of the structure of the Kingdom.

The main factor that caused the rapid creation of ministries and advancement of administrative organizations was the discovery of oil in the eastern province in the 1930s. This discovery and the increased complexity of modern affairs rendered the old administration inadequate.[7] Several administrations were created to cope with such rapid growth. Thus many ministries were created, the Ministry of Foreign Affairs (1930), Ministry of Finance (1932), Ministry of Defense (1944), Ministry of Interior, and the Ministry of Communications (1953). This new Kingdom established diplomatic relations,[8] and then a number of centralized departments were formed

---

[5] *See* Soliman A. Sulaim, *supra* note 3, at 29–30; Ahmed H. Dahlan, *The Saudi Arabian Council of Ministers: its Environment, its Role and its Future, in* Politics, Administration and Development in Saudi Arabia 66–67 (Ahmed H. Dahlan ed., 1990).

[6] *See* Soliman A. Sulaim; *supra* note 3, at 35–39.

[7] *See id.* at 40–42, Richard F. Nyrop, Saudi Arabia: A Country Study, United States Printing Office 59 (1984).

[8] *See* Abdulhakim Altahawi, Al Malik Faisal Wa al Alaqat al Kharigiyah al Saudia [King Faisal and the Saudi Foreign Relation] 34–54 (2002).

and that eventually was the main factor in the establishment of the Council of Ministers.[9]

The Council of Ministers (Majlis Al Wuzara) was established in 1953 by the order of King Abdulaziz. In his father's footsteps, King Saud bin Abdulaziz (1953–1964) held the first session for the Council of Ministers in March of 1954. At its foundation the Council of Ministers only served as an advisory body. In 1958 Crown Prince Faisal bin Abdulaziz, as Prime Minister, transformed the Council into a legislative administrative body with decision-making abilities. Almost all of the constitutional basics were embedded in the law of the Council of Ministers. Crown Prince Faisal made a serious attempt to introduce modern constitutionalism into the Kingdom between 1959 and 1960, but they did not go beyond being proposals. However when he became king, he was able to effect some changes. Most of the ministries, including welfare administrations, developed during King Faisal's Rule (1964–1975), and the Ministry of Justice was established in 1970.[10]

During the rule of King Khalid bin Abdulaziz (1975–1982) the Council of Ministers regulated the policies of the Kingdom. It also formed the state policy in domestic and foreign affairs. The Council also worked on policy making in relation to most public affairs, social welfare, economy, education, and health. The economic boost caused by high oil prices was a big factor in the governmental expansions during that era; a committee was then formed to prepare a new constitution.[11]

Through his awareness of the people's needs and aspirations, King Fahad bin Abdulaziz (1982–2005) was the pioneer in the evolution of the Saudi Constitution. On March 1 of 1992, the Custodian of the two Holy Mosques King Fahad bin Abdulaziz announced three fundamental laws, which constitute the Basic System of Governance, the Consultative Council Law, and the Regional Law.[12]

---

[9] Faisal bin Mishal, *supra* note 1, at 78.

[10] *See* Ahmed H. Dahlan, *supra* note 4, at 72–73; Soliman A. Sulaim, *supra* note 3, at 46–68; Abdulhakim alTahawi, *supra* note 7, at 167–169.

[11] *See* Ahmed H. Dahlan, *supra* note 4, at 74; Ahmad alDa'jani, Khalid bin Abdul Aziz 115–119 (2002); Ahmad H. Dahlan, *supra* note 1, at 127 (1984).

[12] *See* Saudi Arabia The Basic System of Governance, Royal Order No. A/90, (27/8/1412H, Mar. 1, 1992), O.G. Um al Qura No. 3397 (2/9/1412H, Mar. 5, 1992);

The Basic System is what mainly concerns us. It is the most important constitutional document of the three fundamental laws initiated in 1992. It is the document that states that the Quran and the Sunnah of Prophet Muhammad are the Kingdom's constitution.[13] The seventh article of the Basic System states that Islamic Sharia (Islamic Rule) is the main foundation of the Kingdom, the government draws its authority from the Quran and Sunnah, and those two sources govern all administrative regulations of the Kingdom.[14] This stresses that the Kingdom's roles and objectives are to protect and apply the principles of Islam and enforce it.[15] The Basic Law document is led by Islam in defining the responsibilities of the Kingdom, while also defining the relationship between the rulers and the ruled based on brotherhood, consultation and cooperation, and further defining the rule of the land.[16]

In the light of what was mentioned, we notice the importance of applying Islamic law, and the law of Hodud in Saudi Arabia. Any failure to apply even one of the Hodud or any Islamic law would be a major constitutional issue. Islam is the law of the land in Saudi Arabia. The same is said to the moral side of Rahma and Sitr in the law because of the strong command and order to be merciful in the Quran and Sunnah: "Only through the Divine Mercy have you (Muhammad) been able to deal with your followers so gently. If you had been stern and hard-hearted, they would all have deserted you a long time ago. Forgive them and ask God to forgive (their sins) and consult with them in certain matters. But, when you reach a decision, trust God. God loves those who trust Him."[17]

The Regional Law, Royal Order No. A/91 (27/8/1412H, Mar. 1, 1992), O.G. Um al Qura No. 3397 (2/9/1412H, Mar. 5, 1992); The Majlis al Shura. Council Law, Royal Order No. A/91, (27/8/1412H, Mar. 1, 1992), O.G. Um al Qura No. 3397 (2/9/1412H, Mar. 5, 1992).

[13] *See* Saudi Arabia The Basic System of Governance, art. 1.

[14] *See* Saudi Arabia The Basic System of Governance, art 7.

[15] *See* Saudi Arabia The Basic System of Governance, art 23.

[16] *See* The Custodian of the holy mosques' Fahd bin Abdulaziz, Speech on the Issuance of the Basic Law of Governance (Mar. 11, 1992); Prince Saud Alfaisal, Saudi Minister of Foreign Affairs, Address at the World Conference on Human Rights Vienna, Austria (June 15, 1993).

[17] The Quran 3 (Al Imran): 159.

Rahma: The Concept through Sharia

This section will argue that the concept of Rahma is highly constitutional and must not be neglected. It will explain what Rahma is and emphasize its importance through explaining the constitutional texts of Quran and Prophetic Sunnah. Historically the Prophet then the Mujtahids (Islamic Scholars) always kept the moral values of the religion in their minds when translating texts that relate to legal matters of daily life, and even when translating how the Hudod should be applied. This was through Prophet Mohammed's (peace be upon him) reported conduct in the application of Sharia and his moral values.

I must emphasize that when reading any verse in Quran as a Muslim we start with the phrase: (Bism Allah AL Rahman Al Raheem) "in the name of God the most gracious, the most merciful."[18] The nouns Rahman and Raheem are from the source of the word Rahma, which has lots of gracious meanings of compassion, love, mercy, and clemency. "Ask them, 'who is the owner of the heavens and the earth? Say: Unto God. He hath prescribed for Himself mercy.'"[19] Rahma is highly constitutional and must be applied. The previous verse indicates that God prescribed for himself mercy. Thus I conclude its prescription in the application of sharia law. Rahma is also decreed when a person repents and reforms from his deviated ways and criminal acts as we will see in the following Quranic verse:

> When faithful come to you, say to them, "Peace be upon you. Your Lord has decreed for Himself to be All-merciful. Anyone of you who commits a sin out of

---

[18] I must note that this is verse 1:1 in the Quran. It is the first sentence in the Quran, basically the Islamic constitution starts with "In the name of God most Gracious most Merciful."

[19] The Quran, 6 (Al An'am): 12.

ignorance, then repents, and reforms himself will find that God is All-forgiving and All-merciful.[20]

In Islam, leaders, governments, and Heads of State have been ordered to forgive and apply mercy as a public policy. We notice this in the following verse:

Those bearers of the throne glorify their Lord with His praise. They believe in Him and ask him to forgive the believers. They say, 'Our Lord, Your mercy and knowledge encompass all things. Forgive those who turn to you in repentance and follow your path. Lord, save them from the torment of hell'[21]

Very importantly in Islam, God is all forgiving, and his forgiveness encompasses all things as he stated in his holy book of Quran: "My torment only afflicts those whom I want to punish, but My mercy encompasses all things."[22] This leads to the conclusion that the constitutional forgiveness in Quran applies to all people without prejudice no matter what religion, race, or sex: "(Mohammed), tell My servants that I am All-forgiving and All-merciful."[23]

After reviewing the previous verses, there is no doubt that the concept of Rahma is highly constitutional and must be applied.

Below is a list of some Hadiths from Sunnah (we can find the following hadiths are similar in concept to what was previously mentioned and self-explanatory):

1. "God says, 'My mercy outstrips my wrath.'"[24]

2. "The Messenger of God kissed (his grandson) Alhassan, the son of 'Ali, while Aqra' bin Habis al-Tamimi was sitting nearby. Aqra' said, 'I have ten children and have not kissed any of them.' The Messenger of God looked at

---

[20] The Quran, 6 (Al An'am): 54.

[21] The Quran, 40 (Ghafir): 7.

[22] The Quran 7 (Al A'raf): 156.

[23] The Quran, 15 (Ahijr): 49.

[24] Sahih Muslim no. 7146, Kitab al-Tawbah. This Hadith is a Qudsi hadith (Jerusalem Hadith). It was when the Prophet spoke to God on the rock in the Golden Dome Mosque that is in front the Aqsa Mosque in Jerusalem.

him and said, He who does not show mercy shall not be shown mercy."[25]

3. "God is not merciful to one who is not merciful to people."[26]

4. "The merciful are shown mercy by the most Merciful. Be merciful to those on earth, and He who is in heaven will be merciful to you. Kinship ties are connecting branches from the Merciful. Whoever maintains them will be maintained by God, and whoever cuts them will be cut off by God."[27]

5. "An old man came looking for the Prophet, and the people were slow in making way for him, so the Prophet said, 'He who is unkind to the young and disrespectful to the old is not one of us.'"[28]

6. Aisha (the wife of the Prophet) said, "The Messenger of God never struck anything with his hand, neither woman nor servant. He only did so while struggling in the path of God. Nor did he ever do harm to a thing such as to take vengeance upon its owner. He only did so when God's sacred bounds were violated, and would take vengeance for God."[29]

7. "If the believer knew the punishment of God, he would never feel assured of His Garden (Heaven), and if the non-believer knew the mercy of God, he would never despair of His Garden."[30]

8. "God made mercy one hundred parts. He held back ninety-nine parts, and sent down one part to earth. It is from that part that creatures show mercy to each other, such that a mare will lift her hoof over her foal, fearing that she might harm him."[31]

---

[25] Sahih Albukhari no.6063, Kitab Al Adab.
[26] Sahih Muslim no. 6170, Kitab Alfada'il.
[27] Sunan Altirmithi no. 2049, Kitab Albirr wal-Silah.
[28] Sunan Altirmithi no. 2043, Kitab Albirr wal-silah.
[29] Sahih Muslim no. 6195, Kitab Alfada'il.
[30] Sahih Muslim no. 7155, Kitab Altawbah.
[31] Sahih Albukhari no. 6066, Kitab Aladab.

Similar to the Quranic verses, the Hadith proves the constitutionality of mercy in sharia law, and confirms what was previously mentioned in the Quran. In the first hadith, it could be understood that mercy comes before punishment; thus we might feel the urge to go through forgiveness and rehabilitation before applying any punishment. In the third, fourth, and fifth hadith, we notice an order to be clement and understand that we should be merciful in all the means of life. Surely sharia law should be forgiving, yet forgiveness should not be over applied to the point where the laws are never applied. In the sixth hadith we notice the following part: "He only did so when God's sacred bounds were violated, and would take vengeance for God." This means Hudod must be applied, and this is the main topic of this research and how mercy should come into play. The seventh hadith talks about balancing mercy and punishment. It could be considered vague, but the vagueness of such texts is part of what enable sharia law to evolve and gives avenues for forgiveness. The best way to describe the eighth hadith is by noting that the one mercy God sent down to earth is like a mother's care to the newly born, her love and compassion and distress if the baby cries. We can also further see examples of how wild animals show mercy to their young, and all that is set in one mercy. How would the ninety-nine be like? Thus I conclude that no matter how merciful we are, we cannot reach that point of mercy that God has prescribed for Himself (knowing that the form of mercy we have is one part of a hundred, so there are ninety-nine parts left). "God made mercy one-hundred parts. He held back ninety-nine parts, and sent down one" *id.*

You might think that the Quran and Sunnah texts previously mentioned are religious in nature and have no legal effect. That view is incorrect. In the previous section I wrote about the legal system in Saudi Arabia. As we know, in Saudi Arabia the Quran and Sunnah constitute the country's constitution. Thus all the Quran and Sunnah texts above are constitutional texts that are mandatory and of the highest authority (legally speaking). The general and specific meanings of the Quran and Sunnah texts play a major role in Sharia law; for example the Quranic Hudod texts clearly specify certain types of actions to be considered criminal actions and punishable. Yet some of them do not have a certain punishment specified in the Quran, nor what is the burden of proof, nor how to resolve ambiguity. Thus I am going to focus on the first fundamental concept in interpreting the Islamic constitution (The Quran and Sunnah), which is Rahma.

In the Arabic language, Rahma means mercy, leniency, compassion, and forgiveness.[32] In the Sunnah, the Prophet (peace be upon him) stated that God's mercy came before his wrath and that God is more lenient on the souls of His servants than a mother on her newly born.[33] The Prophet in his conduct as a Prophet and judge, and the highest authority in translating the meanings of the Quran, whenever presented with an issue and/or was asked to choose between two solutions for an issue chose (Arham al amryan wa aysarahum) the most merciful and easiest to be fulfilled of the two choices. For example, when the Prophet (peace be upon him) conquered Makkah, he asked Omar bin Alkhattab to send for some of the known leaders and generals in Makkah. Omar thought that the Prophet wanted to try them, and Omar said, "I will teach them a lesson." The Prophet instead called on them to tell them they were safe and forgiven, and read the following verse:

> They said, 'We swear by God that he has given preference to you over us and we have sinned' (Joseph) said, 'No one will blame you on this day. God will forgive you; He is more Merciful than others.'[34]

This was an example on how the prophet always chose the most merciful and easiest conduct to resolve an issue.[35]

Thus I conclude that Rahma is one of the major keys in translating the meaning of the Quran and Sunnah and must be always in our in prospective when dealing with new issues never dealt with and in the application of Hudod. But it should not act as a repellent from the application of Hudod; it should be considered a major guideline because there is no joy or satisfaction in the application of Hodud. It is also noticed that Sharia law strongly urges the people to be clement and also mandates forgiveness in government policies.

---

[32] I am defining the word Rahma as a native Arabic speaker: we can say that Rahma is a mercy and leniency that is accompanied with strong compassion that compels a person to do-good and be lenient in his acts and conducts. It could also be defined as a feeling/urge from the heart that is compelling a person to be lenient in action, and change the surroundings of another person in agony, and change the action to have a less devastating effect or not have any devastating effect.

[33] Sahih Albukhari 2235/5 no 5653. http://ejabat.google.com/ejabat/thread?tid=2d625c99f6b1044f

[34] The Quran 12 (Joseph): 91, 92.

[35] http://www.burhanukum.com/article142.html. Last visited on 20/4/2012 7:00 p.m.

The Hudod

In this section I will give the general definition of Hudod and go on to define every single Hudd. In doing so I will prove that the Hudod crimes have been defined carefully to fit a small amount of acts to be Hudod crimes in order to prove that under the rigid form of Hodud law lays a strong emphasis on Rahma and a methodology of application based on mercy (Dar'a Alhodud bil shubuhat).

The Definition of Hodud in the Arabic Dictionary of Lisan Al Arab (The Arabian Tongue)

The word's origin is Hudd, and it means the separation between two things, a border. The legal Hodud separate between the permissible and impermissible. Some of the impermissible are considered Fawahish (Fawahish: of such audacity); they are not to be approached at all. These are what we consider Hudod Allah (The limits set by God) as referred by the Quran: "Those are the Limits set by Allah, approach not nigh."[36]

The Jurists' Opinion on the Definition of Hodud (The Four Major Scholars of Islam)

It is important to properly define Hudod in Sharia Law. When there are different opinions between scholars, a person is free to choose one of the opinions.

---

[36] The Quran, 2 Surat Albaqara (The Cow): 187. The ayah specifically did not talk about the Hudod. The verse mostly talks about Fasting and how to have sexual relations with your wife during Ramadan. I must say that the lisan Al arab dictionary uses the Quranic verse to express the meaning and uses of the word.

Imam Mālik b. Anas, was once invited to have his legal judgments enforced by the Caliph Harūn al-Rashīd, however he thoughtfully declined stating: "O Commander of the Faithful. Verily the differences of the scholars are a mercy from Allah to this nation. Each follows what is correct in his view, each is on guidance, [and] each desires Allah." The other famous Imams are reported to have said similar statements of tolerance.[37]

This is the consensus of the Muslim jurists.[38] When looking to the differences it is important to note that these differences give room to a more merciful means of action, as in to define a crime in a

---

[37] http://ibrahimlong.com/2010/04/29/41/. Posted on April 29, 2010by Ibrahim J. Long. This Article is very informative on the history of the traditional schools of Sharia law. He states the following relative info on the history of the traditional schools, and how it emerged:

> Sacred Law does not only entail the Qur'ān and the Sunnah, it also includes within it methodologies for their interpretation and application. While each school of Sacred Law considers the Qur'ān and the Sunnah as possessing divine legal authority, they also recognize that to derive the rulings from this authority demands the use of human intellect. The first to use his intellect was the Prophet himself (peace and blessings be upon him), and then his companions (may Allah be pleased with them all). During the Prophet's lifetime he was available to correct, affirm, or reject the legal reasoning of those around him; however after he passed away (peace and blessings be upon him) the interpretation of Sacred Law fell into the hands of his companions. Many refrained from this arduous task, yet those most qualified made judgments based upon consensus, a more qualified scholar's opinion, or their own legal reasoning. At present judicial principles have been derived through their own and their students' understanding of Sacred Law and codified in four legal schools: Ḥanafī, Mālikī, Shāfiī, and Ḥanbalī. Though differences are present the consensus of the Muslim Community (al-ummah) has recognized them as valid and obligated pious Muslims to follow one in his or her daily life.

[38] http://www.passia.org/meetings/rsunit/Islamic-Schools-Jurisprudence.htm.   Last visited 5/16/2012 4 p.m. An Article by Prof. Abdulrahman Abad that states that the main reason for the freedom of choice, when the major Muslim jurists have different opinions, lays on the fact that all the jurists have a correct methodology that bases their opinions on a correct verse in Quran & Sunnah. This opinion is according to the following Sunnah hadith: "Religion is merciful, effortless and simple" *sahih Albukari Kitab Al Iman bab aldeen yusr.*

way in favor of minimizing the scope of jurisdiction. The Hudod are specific crimes that have been defined precisely.

a)   **The Shafi'yi Definition:**

The general meaning of the word "Hudd" is to forbid, and we could say that this may be the reason a gate guard is called Huddad because he forbids the unwanted from entering. The Arabic noun for Iron is Hadid, it was called Hadid because it forbid weapons from reaching who ever had an iron shield on. Hence, the Hudd of anything is what keeps foreign elements from becoming integral parts. Hudd in Sharia, is what forbids the criminal from repeating the offence.[39]

b)   **The Hanafys' Definition:**

In the Al Dur Al Mukhtar book we have the following definition: The Hudd in the Arabic language is a prohibition, and in legal definition, it is a fixed punishment, which is a right belonging to God as a deterrence.[40] Ibn Abdin further elaborates on the previous statement, and emphasizes the fixed nature of the Hudd, and adds that it is fixed in nature and amount, such as mode of execution and number of lashes.[41]

The Kasani definition: Hudd is a fixed punishment as a right belonging to God. It is different from Tazeer (flexible and undetermined punishment), which can be flogging, imprisonment, or other punishments. The Hudd is different from Qisas (to retaliate or make return for a wrong injury with like) because in the case of Qisas it is a right belonging to the person, and as a person he can forgive it or make reconciliation.[42]

---

[39] Mohammed Ahmad Al Rakbi, Alnathm Almusdhdhab Fi Sharh Gharib Almuhathab, Published with Abi Izac Al Shirazi, Almuhadhdhab, (Egypt Dar Ihya Al kutub Al' Arabia n.d) Vol. 2, pp. 264–267.

[40] Al Dur Almukhtar Sharh Tanweer Al Absar, Published with Ibn Abdeen, Hashiat Radd Almuhtar (Egypt: Dar Alfikr, 1979) Vol.4, p. 3.

[41] Ibn Abdeen Hashiat Radd Almuhtar (Egypt: Dar Alfikr, 1979) Vol. 4, p. 3.

[42] Al'a Aldeen Kasani, Badai' Alsanai' (Beirut: Dar Alkatib Al arabi, 1982) Vol. 7, pp. 33–34.

Ibn Nujaim definition was the same as the Kasani definition, but he added a note. He viewed Qisas as a Hudd because it is a prescribed and fixed punishment.[43] If this definition was to be accepted then the Hodud are to be of two kinds: one in which forgiveness is acceptable (i.e. Qisas) and the other in which no change of punishment is possible. The majority of the jurists differentiate between Qisas and Hodud. Qisas is the eye-for-an-eye concept in Sharia. The jurists say that it is a right to the aggrieved party and it is left totally to the parties and it may be dismissed anytime even if the case was brought in front of the court, as long as the aggrieved party grants forgiveness. In Qisas, mercy is applicable on any level even after the judgment is passed (e.g. if a person is convicted of murder, the aggrieved can forgive, and the death penalty shall not be applied). This applies even if forgiveness was granted seconds before the administration of the penalty. The Hudod crimes are rights to God and public necessities. Thus when a case reaches the court, intercession and forgiveness is banned. This is the basis that differentiates between Qisas and Hudod.

c)   **The Malikiyah Definition:**

Maliki books did not define the word Hudd as others did. This was because their source, "Mukhtasar Khalil," did not start with a definition of the word. A relative definition in the Maliki School is Al Qurtubi's (well-known maliki jurist) definition; he says: "The hudud are the border lines and the Hudd is an interdiction. This is why iron is called Hadid because it interdicts weapons from reaching the body of the person wearing iron armor, and a guardsman is called Huddad because of his power to forbid. Thus the Hodud punishments are called Hodud because they act as deterrence and forbid the commitment of the Hodud.... When God communicated the rules of marriage and divorce, he described them saying: "Those are the Hodud

---

[43] Zain Al Din Ibn Nujaim, Albahr Al Raiq Sharh Kanz Al daqauq (Pakistan: Al Mutba'ah Al'Arabiyya n.d) Vol. 5, p. 2. Zain Al Din Ibn Nujaim, Albahr Al Raiq Sharh Kanz Al daqauq (Pakistan: Al Mutba'ah Al'Arabiyya n.d) Vol. 5, p. 2.

of God," to which he commanded obedience. He then goes on with his definitions to conclude that those who transgress the Hodud are wrong doers".[44]

d) **The Hanabilah Definition:**

The definitions by Hanbali jurists are the same as Hanafi jurists. Al Bahuti stresses that the Hodud are prescribed and fixed, and they are not open for any adjustment or alterations.[45]

Thus in conclusion, the word Hodud has two meanings. The first meaning is that it is a prescribed and fixed prohibition that is in accordance with the legal maxim "no crime or punishment without a text," and that is so as everybody knows what is permissible and impermissible and behaves accordingly. The Quran says, "(The believers) who repent for their sins, worship God, praise Him, travel through the land (for pious purposes), kneel down and prostrate themselves in obedience to God, make others do good and prevent them from sins and abide by the laws of God, will receive a great reward. Let this be glad news for the believer."[46] The second is that the Hudod are fixed punishments prescribed for violating the particular crimes of Hudod. This meaning is clearly viewed in the Prophet's (peace be upon him) Statement reproving Osamah bin Zaid when he interceded in a Hudd punishment. The Prophet (peace be upon him) said: "Do you intercede in a Hudd belonging to God?" all the Hudod are pure rights belonging to God because they are promulgated for the protection of the society against crimes that affect the society's well-being. Therefore they are determined as

---

[44] Abu Abdullah Mohammed Ahmed Alansari Al Qurtubi, Aljami' li ahkam al Quran (Riyadh: Maktabat Al Riyadh al Hadithah, 1372/1952), Vol. 2, pp. 145–337. "Tafseer Al Qurtubi."

[45] See:
  1- Sharaf aldin al maqdasi, Al iqna' (Beirut: Dar al Ma'rifah n.d), Vol. 3, p. 244.
  2- Mansour Al Bahuti, Kashshaf Alqina' 'an matn Aliqna' (Beirut: Dar al Fikr, 1982), Vol. 6, p. 77.
  3- Abdelqadir Alshaybani, Nayl Almatalib Be Sharh Dalil Altalib (Kuwait: Maktabat Al Falah, 1983), Vol. 2, p. 350.
  4- Mar'I Ghayt, Almuntaha fi a jam'a bain al iqna' wal muntaha (Al Riyadh: Al Mu'asasah Al Saudia n.d), 2nd Ed. Vol. 3, p. 296.

[46] The Quran, 9 (Surat Altawbah): 112.

"Huquq lilahi ta'ala" to ensure enforcement. No human intervention is allowed to forgive them or minimize them in any way.[47] In other words the cause of describing the Hodud as a right belonging to Allah is because they are promulgated for the protection of the society, and the protection of property, mind, lineage, honor, and reputation.[48]

1.   Ridda (Apostasy):

The Hadd of Ridda or apostasy is very controversial. I will argue in this section that although this Hudd is recognized as a crime, the Quran never established a penalty for it.

There is no compulsion into Islam because compulsion is not compatible with the essence of the Islamic faith and free will. But once Islam is accepted, turning back is an act of Kufr (non-believers and Apostates) is condemned by Quran as a Hudd and warns of grievous consequences.

> (Mohammed), they ask you about fighting in the sacred month. Tell them that it is a great sin. However, creating an obstacle in the way of God, disbelief in Him and the sacred mosque, and driving away the neighbors of the sacred mosque is an even greater sin in the sight of God; disbelief in God is worse than committing murder. (The pagans) Still try to fight you to make you give up your religion. The deeds in this Life of those of you who give their religion and who die disbelievers will be made void and in the life hereafter. These people will be the dwellers of hell wherein they will remain forever.[49]

It is obvious that the Ayah (Quranic verse) mentions no fixed punishment. It is the Sunnah that prescribed, in unambiguous terms, death as a Hudd punishment for apostasy. The hadith conveying the death penalty was reported by Ibn Abbas that the Prophet said, "Whoever abandons his religion should be killed."[50]

---

[47] Badai' Al Sanai', Vol. 7, p. 56.
[48] Hashiat Radd Almuhtar, Vol. 4, p. 3.
[49] Quran, 2 (surat albaqara): 217.
[50] Sahih Albukhari, Vol. 8, pp. 50,163.

A precedent in which this Hudd was implemented by two reputed companions of the prophet was reported when Abu Musa and Muath bin Jabal were sent to Yemen as emissaries (during the early days of Islam). One day during their mission, Muath visited Abu Musa's camp and saw a man tied up. He was told that the man was an apostate; Muath then insisted that he would not set foot on camp until the man was killed. He declared the death penalty as the ruling of God and His messenger.[51] I note that the case was under Muath's order. There was no reported case in Madinah.

The only well reported hadith (teaching of the Prophet [peace be upon him] from Sunnah) with a high degree of authenticity was reported by Othman bin Affan that the Prophet (peace be upon him) said:

> No Muslim witnessing that there is no god but God and Mohammed is His messenger is to be killed except in three cases: a self for a self (murder), the married adulterer, and the one who departs from the religion and abandons the Jama'ah (Society he lives with).[52]

In conclusion, we notice that nowhere in the Quran have we found a verse stating the death penalty to an apostate, and the only high level authenticity hadith accompanies apostasy with abandoning the Jama'ah. When we take a deeper look into the wording of the hadith we notice it says "and the Jama'ah," not and/or, thus the Hudd of Ridda more likely looks to be a Hudd for treason and how to deal with treason. Some Islamic scholars distinguish between apostasy on a personal level, which is not punishable by death, and apostasy that is accompanied with high treason (which was stated in the previous Hadith as Abandoning the Jama'ah, in which case the punishment is for high treason, not

---

The Arabic word used in the hadith for Abandon was 'baddala" which means to exchange something with something else in its place.

[51] Sunan Abid Dawoud "Kitab Alhodud", Vol. 4, p. 127.

[52] Sahih Albukhari, Vol. 8, p. 38

for apostasy).[53] This was according to the following Quranic verses:

> Had your Lord wished, the whole of mankind would have believed in Him. (Mohammed), do you force people to have faith?[54]

> Say, 'Truth comes from your Lord. Let people have faith or disbelieve as they chose.'[55]

> (Mohammed), if they turn away from your message, know that we have not sent you as their keeper. Your duty is only to deliver the message.[56]

> God will not forgive or guide to the right path those who first believe, then disbelieve, again believe and disbelieve, and then increase their disbelief.[57]

These verses again show a room for interpretation that Ridda should not be applied for the mere act of apostasy; Ridda has a treason factor to it. It must be noted that Hanbali jurist Ibn Taymiyyah (1263–1328), held that apostasy carries no legal punishment.

2.   **Stealing "Hudd Alsarika":**

I will argue that due to the strong emphasis on mercy in Sharia law stealing is defined in a nature to be very precise or even narrowly, as to punish stealing not petty theft, and exclude forms of theft to be able to administer a more merciful means of punishment for stealing. I will also shed some light on Islamic theories of reasons that block the application of the penalty. The first thought that might come into any person's mind when talking about stealing in Islamic

---

[53] http://theamericanmuslim.org/tam.php/features/articles/fatwa_freedom_of_belief_minority_rights_in_muslim_countries.
[54] The Quran, 10 (Surat Yunis): 99.
[55] The Quran, 18 (Surat Alkahf): 29.
[56] The Quran, 42 (Surat Alshura): 48.
[57] The Quran, 4 (Surat Alnisa'a): 137.

law is chopping off hands. Although it is true that is the penalty for stealing, many lack the knowledge of what is defined to be stealing (Sarika) in Islamic law. With a more clear understanding they will see that Sharia's apparently tough law has a large general sense of mercy.

Islamic law greatly upholds the holiness and blesses the right of ownership. This must be protected and owners must have a real sense of security for the safety of their money, valuables, and all their goods and belongings. This was through the Quranic verse:

> Believers do not exchange your property in wrongful ways unless it is in trade by mutual agreement. Do not kill one another. God is All-merciful to you.[58]

To achieve this goal and in order to keep civil society together in peace and harmony, the stiff punishment for theft was laid down in the Quranic verse:

> Cut off the hands of a male or female thief as a punishment for their deed and a lesson for them from God. God is Majestic and all-wise. However, God will accept the repentance of whoever repents and reforms himself after committing injustice; He is All-forgiving and All-merciful.[59]

If we take a look at the previous verses mentioned, we notice that the first Ayah contained a general prohibition not to covet and take the properties of others, and that the transfer of ownership can only occur through legal means. All acts of disobedience are punishable, but the punishment for theft, which is a harsh form of criminal appropriation, is a fixed Hudd, as seen in the second Quranic verse previously mentioned. Yes it sounds grave and demanding of punishment, but then when we look at the Prophetic Sunnah, we find six conditions contingent for the implementation of the Sarika Hudd. If any

---

[58] The Quran, 4 (Surat Alnisa): 29.
[59] The Quran. 5 (surat al ma'idah): 38, 39.

one of these conditions is missing, then the Hudd will not be applied. When a condition is missing, there is no Hudd, and a Tazeer punishment is in play. The Tazeer punishment will be met in accordance to the degree of criminality in each case. The Sunnah indicates the cutting point on the hand and the ruling in case of repetition. And the six conditions are:

1. The act of stealing should be committed in stealth (e.g. pick pocketing on a small scale, or if you could imagine a larger scale in the movie Ocean's Eleven). If the act was not concealed, then no Sarika Hudd and therefore no amputation of the hand is required, as if to take the money on the face of dominance and oppression at the sight of people, or by mugging and use of force, because the owner of the money could seek help or fend him off.

2. The stolen object should be valuable in essence, and be of known value. Sentimental value is excluded. (e.g. A baseball signed by Derek Jeter has no value at all in Islamic law, unless it was a known commodity to the community it is in.) Alcohol and drugs are not legal; so if stolen, then there is no Hudd demanded.

3. The Nisab—or minimum limit of amount to be considered a Sarika Hudd—of the item stolen, which is three Islamic Dirhams or a quarter of an Islamic dinar, or an equivalent from other currency. An important factor is this scale is over 1420 years old, and when applying it we should take into factor the buying power of that amount to see what is to be considered an equivalent today. Some might say we weigh the Dirhams (Dirhams are gold coins), and they are an approximate of 4.25 grams, which cost $322. But this fails to look to the factor of the buying power of the Dirham in 690 AD. I really think this measure should be revised to include the buying power of such Dirhams.

4. The theft should be from a Hirz (a usual place where the commodity/money should be kept safely), e.g. where people are keeping their money, such as a bank, where large amounts of money are kept safely. Nowadays it is impractical and illogical that a person would keep ten million

dollars in a safe at home, therefore it is not considered as a Hirz. Another example of a Hirz, would be parking a car in a safe place, locked and with the windows shut.

5.   The theft has to be proven by two witnesses (in accordance with Islamic law on witnesses. Islamic law has strict regulations on who is a valid witness.), or by the thieves confession.

6.   The Claimant of the stolen money must pursue and demand his money through the correct means (e.g. by informing the police of the theft), so if he does not pursue justice, there is no Sarika Hudd and no amputation of the hand.[60]

In summary, yes it is a harsh conviction and penalty if the Sarika Hudd is proven, yet the criteria is so precise that it only punishes a limited number of people. This is because in Islamic law there is no happiness in applying the Hudod. In Prophetic hadith the Prophet says, "Try to find technicalities as not to apply the Hodud as much as you can." The Rahma side of this is the preciseness of the act of stealing and conditions, but it is still possible to be convicted, that possibility acts as deterrence because of the grave penalty if convicted, and it applies in a limited number of cases. It also is possible in a rare circumstance to stop applying the Hudd on the Islamic technicality of "necessity allows the impermissible." The caliphate Omar bin Alkhuttab (one of the strictest jurists and justice oriented caliphates, which didn't premise any way of dealing outside the realm of the Quran and Sunnah) stopped applying the Sarika Hudd in the year of the Ramadah. (It was a year of great hunger and poverty.) This truly shows the room for mercy and one of the greatest Islamic caliphates applying an emergency code for the circumstances of the Ramadah year.[61]

---

[60] http://islamqa.info/ar/ref/9935. Last visited 3/15/2012 at 6:00 p.m.

[61] http://www.islamstory.com/%D8%AA%D8%B7%D8%A8%D9%8A%D9%82-%D8%A7%D9%84%D8%B4%D8%B1%D9%8A%D8%B9%D8%A9. Last visited on 3/9/2012 4:00 a.m.

3. **Drinking Alcohol "Hudd Shurb Alkhamr":**

I will define the Hudd of drinking alcohol and talk about its punishment, to prove that Islam does not mandate the application of lashes on alcohol consumers. Consuming alcohol is a Hudd crime in Islamic Law. Although it is a Hudd crime, again we find that this crime has no specific punishment, similar to the case of the Ridda Hudd. In pre-Islamic Arabia and early years of Islam, consuming intoxicants and drinking alcohol was a well-established factor of enjoyment when mingling socially, that sudden cessation of it would have caused havoc in the community. A gradual legislation was adopted by a series of steps, which in time ended in total prohibition. This gradual legislation was revealed through Quran in the following verses:

> (Mohammed), they ask you about wine and gambling. Tell them that there is a great sin in them. Although they have benefits for men, the sin therein is far greater than the benefit. They ask about what they should give for the cause of God. Tell them, 'Let it be what you can spare.' This is how God explains for you His guidance so that perhaps you will think.[62]

> Believers, do not pray when you are drunk, but instead wait until you can understand what you say.[63]

> Believers, wine, gambling, the stone altars and arrows (that the pagans associate with certain divine characters) are all abominable acts associated with satanic activities. Avoid them so that you may have everlasting happiness. Satan wants to induce hostility and hatred among you through wine and gambling

---

[62] The Quran, 2 (surat albaqarah): 219. In this verse we notice it does not ban the consumption of alcohol it states a reality of benefits and harm, but the harms are more severe than the benefits. The meaning of Khamr: Alcohol.

[63] The Quran, 4 (Surah Alnisa'): 43. In this verse drunkenness is proscribed as unbecoming and not a conduct of a true believer in a state of worship.

and to prevent you from remembering God and prayer. Will you then avoid such things?[64]

As previously mentioned, there is no prescribed punishment for consuming intoxicants in the Quran. Unambiguous Sunnah Hadith prescribed punishment without fixing a number of lashes or method; it would sometimes be lashes or hitting with bare hands or insulting and sometimes an order to make the drinker/drunk cry. The punishment was implemented several times during the lifetime of the Prophet (peace be upon him).

Non-Muslims are not punished for drinking or drunkenness as long as they do it privately. Non-Muslims are only punished for public drinking and drunkenness; such behavior is not tolerated in the Islamic society. The punishment would not be under Hodud jurisdiction; it would be under Tazeer. The Islamic state has respected their religious freedom; they must in return respect the society and its moral standards.

No Muslim or legal authority has any right to spy on any citizen, Muslim or non-Muslims, in his home or any legal private place, even if they had reason to know that he or she is drinking or drunk. Alhakim reported that a man came to Abdullah bin Mas'ud and told him that Walid bin Uqbah's beard was dripping wine. Ibn Mas'ud said: "The prophet forbade us from spying, if he reveals it, we will certainly deal with him."[65] Another incident was when Abdulrahman bin Awf was with Caliphate Omar bin Alkhattab (Alfaroq) patrolling Madinah one night and they saw a light from a house. When they reached the house, they found a closed door and loud voices inside (red-light district kind of night) then the following dialogue arose:

---

[64] The Quran, 5 (Surah Alma'idah): 90, 91. These verses are a clear-cut prohibition but still reason it. It was reported that when these verses were revealed, all of the city of Madinah that day spilled the wine into the streets, and those raising their cups of wine to drink and toast spit them out and spilled them on the floor until the streets were drenched in wine.

[65] Al Mustadrak "Kitab Alhudud", Vol. 4, p. 377. The hadith is said to be Sahih but never reported in Bukhari and Muslim.

Omar: Do you know whose house is this?

Abdulrahaman: No.

Omar: This house is the house of Rubi'ah bin Umayah bin Khalaf, and they are now drinking. What do you think we should do?

Abdulrahman: I think we have violated God's prohibition. God prohibited us from spying, and we are now spying.

Omar immediately heeded the advice and left.[66]

From the previous story we notice a lot of technicalities that prohibit the application of Hudud, like the well-known Islamic theory of "whatever that is structured on illegal standards or falsehood is considered false."

We now know that there is no specific punishment set by Hodud, but the Ijma'a of the Islamic scholars is on eighty lashes. There is still some room to introduce new methods of punishment. As previously mentioned the punishment was not uniform it ranged from an order to make the culprit cry to hitting with hands and lashing. So it may be possible to introduce other methods of punishment that would satisfy at the least the Prophet's (peace be upon him) order to make the Sharib Alkamr cry, like revoking the person's driver license or a heavy fine for first offenders. We also notice a general sense of Sitr (respect for a person's reputation in the community); we notice that info acquired by spying is

---

[66] Almustadrak "Kitab al hudud", Vol. 4, p. 377–382. Alhakim says that the hadith satisfies the requirement of Bukhari and Muslim. I truly think that spying for Khalwa or zina is an un-Islamic practice failing under the same prohibition declared by God and His messenger, and understood by the most reputed companion, including Caliphat Omar. Further more, in the Quran in Ayah 19 of surat alnur: "For those who love to publicize the discreditable happenings among the believers is a severe and humiliating chastisement in this world and in the hereafter verily God knows (The innermost truth of everything) and you do not." The Prophet Said: Whoever veils his Muslim brother's awrah (discreditable act), God will veil his arah in the hereafter. And whoever unveils his Muslim brother's awrah, God will unveil his awrah until he scandalizes him with it (even if he commits it) in the innermost part of his own home. *Sunan Ibn Majah "kitab alhudod",* Vol. 2, p. 850.

deemed useless according to sharia law. These refined theories try to limit the application of the Hodud because, I repeat again, there is no joy or satisfaction in its application, and it is a sad day whenever a person is convicted.

4.   Armed Assault and Robbery "Alhiraba":

I will define the hudd of Alhiraba and talk about the choices in the punishment applicable for committing this Hudd to prove how this Hudd can be applied to mandate a more lenient punishment of imprisonment for forceful stealing. This Hudd plays a strategic role in giving room to courts and scholars as to define this Hudd in a way that forceful stealing is under its jurisdiction, in that an alternative punishment of imprisonment can be applied for other methods of stealing other than stealing in stealth. The prohibition of this crime comes from the Quranic Ayah:

> The only proper recompense for those who fight against God and His messenger and try to spread evil in the land is to be killed, crucified, or either to have one of their hands and feet cut from the opposite side or to be sent into exile. These are to disgrace them in this life and they will suffer a great torment in the life hereafter.[67]

The term Hirabah involves several crimes. It includes the criminal act of taking property of another against his will by violence or intimidation, which is called "armed robbery." It also covers any act of terrorism, even if there was no physical harm or taking of the property. In general it covers the causing and spread of corruption on earth, such as the poisoning of drinking water, or by wreaking havoc and bombing, and causing great criminal damage to the state security and/or economy.

In this Hudd we notice that the Quran gave the courts the choice between numerous penalties if the case was proven. The courts have the option to execute, crucify, cut the culprits right hand and left foot or the opposite, or banish him/her from the

---

[67] The Quran, 5 (Surat alma'idah): 33.

lands, which is equivalent to imprisonment. An alternative punishment of imprisonment can be applied for stealing that does not go under the Hudd of Sarika.

An important point is that Tawbah (regret for doing the crime with a belief as not to go back to it) repent of the committer of the Hudd of Hiraba relieves him of the punishment. The majority of jurists express an exception in the Tawbah of the Muharib (terrorists, rebels, any warriors known as warriors of a state or of a group or organization, e.g. mafia members), which is qualified by his willing surrender to the authorities before capture or arrest it relieves him from the Hudd punishment,[68] but a Tazeer can be applied (e.g Prince Mohammed bin Naif's rehabilitation program for terrorist who surrender themselves).[69]

5.   **Adultery (Hudd Al-Zina):**

I will define the Hudd of Zina and talk about the burden of proof in this Hudd to prove that the only way this Hudd could be applied is through confession; although it is possible it could be applied through other means, it is a practical impossibility. The prohibition of Zina (illicit sexual intercourse) and the Hudd punishment Ghair Almuhsan (person who never married or not married yet) originate from the Quran. The prohibition of the act was instant, but the punishment came in two stages. A really short ayah severely condemned Zina as a Fahisha (an extremely abnormal and corrupt behavior). It is a dreadful quest that opens the path to many evils, such as hazardous health problems plaguing our world today. In many instances it resulted in murders, feuds, or loss of reputation and property. Thus prohibition and punishment are manifested as divine will in the following Ayat (verses): "Do not even approach adultery. It is indecent and an evil act."[70] There are two types of

---

[68] Hashiat Aldusuqi, Vol. 4, p. 347.

[69] This program is a very innovative program that actually is a Tazeer (A Tazeer is not always an alternative punishment, but considered an alternate mean for a legal a consequence and rehabilitating. The main reason for application of Tazir is to correct the society.), which pays wages to the family of the Muharib and rehabilitates the person to be reintroduced into the community without the anguish of starting from zero and suffering from the consequences of his previous way of life.

[70] The Quran, 17 (Surah Alisra): 32.

punishments for Zina—one is for Ghair Almuhsan (the unmarried), and it is a hundred lashes and in the following Quranic Ayah:

> Flog the fornicateress and the fornicator with a hundred lashes each. Let there be no reluctance in enforcing the laws of God, if you have faith in God and the Day of Judgment.[71]

The second type of punishment is for the Muhsan (the married person), which is stoning to death, as he or she has legal means for sexual satisfaction. It also involves the stigma of infidelity in the case of married people. The Prophet (peace be upon him) said:

> The zani muhsan (married person who is convicted with zina) are to be stoned to death, and the ghair almuhsans a hundred lashes and banishment for one year.[72]

The Prophet (peace be upon him) implemented the hudd for zina in several cases. The Ma'az case was a stoning because Ma'az was muhsan. The following dialogue happened:

> Prophet (peace be upon him): are you sure you committed Zina Ma'az? You might have kissed, looked, or even committed something other than Zina?
>
> Ma'az: I am sure I committed Zina.
>
> Prophet (peace be upon him): Is this man crazy? (Asking his companion, they answer back that he is a known sane man) are you sure you committed Zina Ma'az?
>
> Ma'az insists that he committed Zina to the point that the last question the Prophet (peace be upon him) asked him was, "Did you penetrate her?" and Ma'az

---

[71] The Quran, 24 (surah Alnur): 2.
[72] Sunan Altirmithi "Kitab Alhudod", Vol. 4, p. 32.

said, "Yes, I did penetrate her." Then the judgment to stone Ma'az was passed. The companions stoned him, when Ma'az felt the pain of the stones he started running away; the companions caught up and continued stoning until he died. When the news reached the Prophet (peace be upon him), the Prophet expressed regret and said that they could have let him go. The reasoning for that regret is not that he wanted to abandon the Hudd but the Prophet (peace be upon him) wanted to verify more because if Ma'az had took back his confession, the Hudd wouldn't apply.[73] This could probably mean a person's confession can be retracted during any level of court hearings up to the moment of administering the punishment in Hudd cases.

Another issue worth talking about is if the confessor of Zina names his or her lover, the Hudd does not apply to the other person (the lover). It only applies if they confess to it themselves. In the Ma'az case, the lover was named, yet it was never reported that the Prophet (peace be upon him) summoned or questioned her. Abu Dawod wrote in his book a case of a reported hadith. The hadith was about a man who confessed to Zina to the Prophet (peace be upon him) and named a woman as his lover. The Prophet (peace be upon him) sent for the woman, asking her about the incident, but she denied it ever occurred. Thus the man was flogged on his confession, and she was never punished.[74]

To prove Zina in another by means other than confession is very hard, and is a practical impossibility. To prove Zina we need four witnesses that fit the strict criteria of being reliable witness in Islam (e.g. well known for their honesty, never been known to always fall back on their contractual agreements). The four witnesses must all witness the full insertion of the male's penis into the woman's vagina. There is no recorded case of Zina proven through witnesses from the time of the Prophet

---

[73] Tafsir Alqurtubi, Vol. 9, pp. 104–106.
[74] Sunan Abi Dawod "Kitab Alhodud', Vol. 4, p. 159.

(peace be upon him) up to this date because proof is very difficult to establish.[75]

This heavy burden of proof, the Prophet's (peace be upon him) conduct with the confessors, and not applying the Hudd to the people named in the confessions all accumulate and serve to achieve the purposes of Sharia, in the Sharia concepts of Rahma (mercy/forgivness) and Sitr (to conceal and cover).

6.   **Incorrect Accusation of Zina "Slander" (Al-Qathf):**

I will define the Hudd of slander to prove that this Hudd works as a deterrent from accusing people with Zina, and it also upholds the concept of Sitr (conceal the downfalls of other people). This crime is the crime of falsely accusing someone of committing Zina. The accuser must provide four witnesses; each of them must witness Zina the same way previously mentioned. The witnesses are examined separately and rigorously in detail. Any inconsistency in the testimony renders the accusations invalid, and the accusers are sentenced to have committed the Hudd crime of Qathf. This crime is mentioned in the Quran in this verse:

> Those who accuse women[76] of committing adultery—but are not able to prove their accusation by producing four witnesses—must be flogged eighty lashes. Never accept their testimony thereafter because they are sinful. Except that of those who afterwards repent and reform themselves; God is All-forgiving and All-merciful.[77]

This Hudd almost works as a guaranty not to convict somebody with Zina. This is more related to the previous Hudd (Zina). To the point that we have this Hudd concerned with

---

[75] http://www.bt.com.bn/files/digital/Islamia/Issue101/SP4Jun.4.pdf. Last visited. 3/7/2012 at 1:00 a.m.
[76] The Quranic verse uses the following wording for women (Alm'uminat Almuhsanat).
[77] The Quran 24 (surat Alnur): 4, 5.

concealing and saving the peoples' reputations from the repercussions of being falsely accused with Zina.

7.   Dr'a Alhudod Bil Shubuhat (Fending off the Hudud by Suspicions and Technicalities):

The actual meaning of Shubha is anything that would cause uncertainty in the guilt of the person committing the Hudd. It is a known legal principle that doubt is interpreted to the benefit of the accused. Out of compassion and mercy, the Prophet (peace be upon him) draws attention to this principle in retaliation to the harsh Hudod punishments. The Prophet (peace be upon him) said:

> Fend off the Hodud as much as you can. If you can find a way out for them[78] let them go. That is because it is better for the Imam[79] to err in forgiveness than to err in punishment.[80]

Another hadith reported by Abu Hurairah that the Prophet (peace be upon him) said: "Fend off the Hudod whenever you can."[81] Ibn Abbas reported a hadith that the Profit Said: "Fend off the Hodud by the Shubuhat."[82]

The four major scholars of Islam (four major Mathahib)[83] have all discussed the meanings and applications of the Prophet's orders. The strongest advocates to it are the Hanafiyah then the Malikiya, the Shafi'iya, and at last the Hanabilah. It is important to know that when the jurists talk about the shubhat fending off the Hudod, it does not mean that

---

[78] Them: The perpetrators that committed the Hodud.

[79] Imam meaning the leader and ruler of the land or whoever was appointed by him; this hadith was before the theory of separation of powers, which is consistent with the Shariah in a way that the courts of law and judges are the final settlement and say in the Hodud. So the fending off is until before they reach the courts where they would be fully enforceable.

[80] Sunan Altirmithi, "Kitab al hudud", Vol. 4, p. 25.

[81] Sunan Ibn Majah "Kitab Alhudod", Vol. 2, p. 850.

[82] Musnad Abu Hanifah "Musnad Ikrimah wa Muqsim", p. 186.
Shubuhat is the plural of shubha, which means "doubt."

[83] The four major schools/scholars are Hanafi, Maliki, Shafi'I, and Hanbaly.

the offender is let off easily. It is true that the Hudod are fended off by the shubhat, but then a lesser punishment of Tazeer is given in proportion with the proved degree of criminality or immoral act. I will further elaborate on the standard statements of the four major schools of Islam.

1.   The Malikiya:

In a ruling of a case of a grandfather stealing from his grandson, there should be no amputation for the fact that in Qisas the murder of a grandfather to his grandson does not apply the death penalty, only the paying of a severe Diyyah.[84] This was in accordance to the Quranic verse: "No-one should be charged beyond his capacity. A mother should not be made to suffer because of her child, nor should he to whom the child is born (be made to suffer) because of his child. And on the (Father's) heir is incumbent the like of that (which was incumbent on the father)..."[85]

2.   The Shafi'iyah:

Say that the third required circumstance for the implementation of the Hudod is the absence of the shubha, and that is in consistency with the previously mentioned Hadiths.

3.   The Hanafiyah:

"The origin of taking the shubha into consideration here is in a reputed hadith of the Prophet peace and prayers be upon him: 'fend off the Hudod by the shubuhat'. Rationally the Hudd is a full punishment that requires full criminality."[86]

The best example would be imagining a jury, and the jury finds the suspect to be ninety-nine percent liable for the crime. The one percent chance would fend off the Hudd, and a Tazeer would be administered.

---

[84] Diyyah is the blood money paid in the case of murder; in intended murder and semi intended murder a sever diyyah is required.
[85] The Quran, 2 (Surat Albaqara): 233.
[86] Badai Alsanai', Vol.7, p. 34. See Hashiat Radd Almuhtar, Vol. 4, p. 18.

4.   The Hanbalys:

Say that to amputate in theft there must be no shubha at all,[87] and that was in accordance to the previously mentioned hadiths.

Examples of the shubuhat by the jurists:

• The shubha can be related to core elements of the crime (e.g. the thief having a right of acquirement on the stolen property). It is said that no amputation for stealing property owned to an ancestor of the thief no matter how far high of an ancestor is, or how low the descendent is. The shubha in this situation is presumed entitlement to Nafaqah[88] [89](nourishment and care) for the thief.

Another example on having a right invested in the stolen item would be the stealing of a property of a person who owes the thief money. A poor person who steals from an identified Zakat (mandatory amount of money prescribed in Islam to be paid to the needy, and to the avenues of zakat) property on account of his entitlement to it. Thus the hand would not be amputated for the presence of a shubha in the previous examples.[90]

Another statement that is very informative is Albahuti's statement: in amputation for theft, there must be no shubha because of the Messenger's statement God's peace be upon him: "Fend off the Hudod by shubuhat as much as you can." Thus, a father cannot be amputated for stealing his sons' (descendants') property due to the hadith: "You and your property belong to your father." This is applicable to the father, mother, son, daughter, the direct grandfather, or grandmother because of the special close relationship between them that renders testimonies between them inadmissible. Likewise, the son will not have his hand amputated for stealing the property of any of his ancestors.

---

[87] Kashaf Alqina', Vol.6, p. 78.
[88] Nafaqah: Is an entitlement to alimony.
[89] Nihayat Almuhtaj, Vol. 7, p. 444.
[90] Tuhfat Almuhtaj, Vol. 9, p. 131.

But there is amputation in theft between other relatives, such as brothers, sisters, uncles, aunts, nieces, because the relationship here is not as close as to forbid beneficial testimonies among them.[91]

We can also add martial relationship as a shubha that fends of amputation in theft between spouses. Because there is no amputation between spouses in the case of stealing, whether they live in the same house or separate houses, because of the presumption that they enter each other's houses and utilize each other's property.[92]

Sometimes the jurists do not agree on the existence of a shubha, they differ on its strength to fend off a Hudd. An example on that controversy would be stealing from Bait Almal (the place where public money and property are kept, e.g. the treasury). In this case Alshirazy says: "If a thief steals from bait almal, he will not suffer amputation because it was reported that one of the province rulers wrote to Omar asking him about theft from bait almal. Omar replied that there was no amputation because every Muslim had a right invested in it". It was also reported that a man stole from bait almal and Ali bin abutalib (The fourth caliphate and the Prophets nephew) ruled out amputation as the thief had a share in it.[93] The Malikiya agreed in the existence of the shubha in the previous case, but dismissed it as being very weak that it could not fend off the Hudd. They said: "The thief will be cut if the shubhah is weak such as stealing from bait almal."[94] Ibn Alhumam says: "The Shafi'i's opinion is that the thief will not be cut if he steals from bait almal. Almaliki contradicts him by saying that bait almal is a sacred property, and he has no right to it before his need, so he will be cut as a Hudd crime. Our opinion is that it is a property belonging to the public and he is one of them.

---

[91] Kashaf Akqina', Vol. 6, p.141. See Nayl almaarib, Vol. 2, p. 374.
[92] Badai Alsanai, Vol. 7, p. 75.
[93] Almuhadhdhab, Vol. 2, p. 281.
[94] Munah Al Jalil, (Beirut: Dar alfikr, n.d.), Vol. 9, p. 306. See Al Khurashi Ala Mukhtasa Khalil, (Beirut: Dar Alfikr, n.d.), Vol. 7, p. 96.

That is also the opinion of caliphates Omar and Ali, so he should not be cut."[95]

- A Shubha can also be in the mens rea.[96] We can see an example in the following Shafi'i view: If a man finds a woman in his bed and in a mix up mistakes her for his wife and makes love to her, there will be no Hudd of Zina if his claim of mistake is strong and proven.[97] Another similar example, some marriages were conducted without the husband seeing his wife till the night of the marriage, if he was newly married and a woman was misguidedly sent to him as his bride and he sleeps with her, there will be no Hudd.[98]

- A Shubha can also arise when there is a fractional satisfaction of the legal requirements, such as marrying a woman without legal witnesses (mandatory in Islamic marriage contracts) and having sexual intercourse with her, there is no Hudd for the shubha of marriage.[99] But if a person marries a fifth wife, and has five wives at the same time, there will be no shubha to fend off the Hudd because the prohibition and limitation not to marry more than four wives in Islam is well known.[100]

- A shubha can also be found when there is a conflict of evidence that would result in doubt. The best example to give would be Alnawawy's example if four men testified against a woman that she committed Zina and four women testified that she was a virgin, neither she nor her slanderers would be punished.[101] Alshirazi elaborates on the previous example, that she would not be punished because of her imperforated hymen indicated the physical state of not having experienced

---

[95] Fatah alqadeer, Vol. 5, p. 376. See Almubsut, Vol. 9, p. 188.
[96] The guilty mind, or criminal intent.
[97] Almuhadhdhab, Vol. 2, p. 268.
[98] Kashaf Alqina', Vol. 6, p. 78.
[99] Hashiat Radd Almuhtar, Vol. 4, p. 24. See Alhidaya, Sharh Bidayat Almubtadi, (Egypt: Mustafa Albabi Alhalabi Press, n.d.), Vol. 1, p. 100.
[100] ID. pp. 316–317.
[101] Mughni Almuhtaj, Vol. 4, p. 151.

sexual penetration.[102] But the shubhah would crumble as in Albulqini's explanation that if the woman was found Ghawra' [103] (Ghawra: deeply situated hymen).

The Malikis discussed the same hypothetical issue of a woman being ghawra'. Some of them supported a notion of shubha capable of fending off the Hudd, and some supported the idea that she could be ghawra', which would make the testimonies of the Zina witnesses valid.[104]

We notice that the Shubuhat theory gives great flexibility in the law of Hudod to be more merciful. It highlights the factor that in the application of Hodud, the jurists have been minimizing presentation in accordance to the Prophet's (peace be upon him) conduct. They have been doing that and at the same time trying not to over interpret it, to the point where the Hodud does not act as a deterrence from committing the crimes, and contributing to the stability of the community.

I conclude this part of my discussion after reviewing it by the following: First, the Hodud crimes are to a specific measure as to cover a specified crime. Secondly, before applying the Hodud we notice a heavy burden of proof that was based on technicalities and theories with a mindset of Rahma and Sitr of the Prophet then the Caliphates and the Islamic scholars. This shows us that the majority of crimes are subject to Tazeer (discretionary punishment) and are left to be determined by individual societies according to local norms and customs. This allows for a tremendous range of flexibility in the development of the penal system. It is truly remarkable that out of the numerous possible crimes and offenses that may be committed by humans, the Sharia only singled out a few for mandatory punishment (six according to the majority of scholars, and four to others). The remaining offenses, which would form the majority of any legal system, are left to Tazeer.

---

[102] Almuhandhdhab, Vol. 4, pp. 150–152.
[103] Ghawra': with a deeply situated hymen which would remain intact event with penetration or partial penetration.
[104] Hashiat Aldusuqi, Vol. 4, p. 319.

Forgivness and Intercession

Forgiveness

The Islamic criminological system not only prevents crime through deterrence, it also prevents crime through education and other constructive social measures. Let us say that that was not enough and a crime was committed despite all the preventive methods, the Islamic system also attempts a rehabilitative effort before the official arrest, trial, or punishment of the offender. The Islamic system not only allows, it encourages members of the society to have positive sympathy towards the wrongdoers, without imposing procedures that might twist his mind and cause on him the permanent shame of crime. Constructive compassion lays in forgiveness toward the offender. This is possible when the legal nature of the crime permits, and the party concerned accepts to forgive in good conscience. Forgiveness takes place before the case is initiated. All the Hudod crimes are declared to be subject to forgiveness or the efforts to achieve it. This was through the following hadith: "Forgive the hudd among you. But should an established case reach me, punishment is certain."[105] This confirms the case of Sufwan bin Umayah when he visited the Prophet (peace be upon him) in Madinah. While Sufwan was napping using his mantel to rest his head, a thief stole it from under his head. He woke up caught him and brought him to the Prophet (peace be upon him). The thief confessed, and the ruling was for amputation for the Hudd of Sarika. Sufwan felt bad for the man and pleaded for forgiveness; the Prophet (peace be upon him) denied on the notion that he should have forgave him before he brought him. Bringing him to the Prophet meant that he was brought to court, and the case was heard.

---

[105] Almuwata li mailik, Alhodud. Can be found on the following hyper link http://www.yanabi.com/Hadith.aspx?HadithID=26 unde020r clipboard no. 206020.

The Prophet God's (peace be upon him), through the hadith to forgive before a case reached him, knew the pitfalls of human weaknesses. Thus he intended by his call to forgiveness to rescue the offender through the healing act of education, which would give the offender a chance to unravel good attitudes. The utmost important anti-crime sentiment is kindheartedness and compassion, and no act can strongly revive such a sentiment other than a similar act of compassion offered, at tough times, by his fellow human being. Such an action of clemency can restore in the offender the concern for the wellbeing of others and trust in society and people. It would help re-socialize with reinforced internal restraint and prohibition. More like a pledge to self-started rehabilitation and law abidance. The forgiver would be deeply gratified for rescuing an individual and returning him to the right path.

Many people commit crimes for reasons of temperament, Satanic thought, a short horizon, temporary submersion of conscience, a strong urge/lust that causes loss of sexual and/or moral control, a strong surge and wave of anger that may cause the blurting of slanderous words and accusations, or falling into extreme depression then seeking relief in alcohol and drugs. Punishing those who have committed these crimes for the first time, and are in sense victims of inherent human weaknesses, while having a chance to restore their former capacities and correct posture, is blind vindictiveness. It is better if the society was aware of this important humanitarian gesture and did not rush to expose such people (victims of their own weaknesses and crimes) to aversive consequences. I truly believe that this would be a key element to civilized life, way more important than space centers, new tech android phones, or building mile high skyscrapers. Cruelty, spite, and the desire to expose others' weaknesses are barbarisms, the shame of which the Quran and Sunnah seek to clear.

> Those who like to publicize indecency among the believers will face painful torment in this world and in the life to come. God knows what you do not know.[106]

The great virtue and humanitarian spirit of pardoning others is a core element of Islam. It starts as one the greatest attributes of God.

---

[106] The Quran.24 (Surat Alnur): 19.

After repeated Divine graces to Bani Israel and their repeated sins, God continued to forgive: "Afterwards, We forgave you so that you would perhaps appreciate Our favors."[107]

When some of the early believers escaped the battlefield,[108] leaving behind Prophet Mohammed (Peace be upon him), God attributed their timid actions to satanic demoralization and forgave them:

> God knows what the hearts contain. Because of some of your bad deeds, those of you who ran away, when you faced the enemy, were misled by Satan. God forgave you for he is All-forgiving and Forbearing.[109]

The Prophet had been commanded to be an example of constructive and candid forgiveness to all Muslims. "Have forgiveness, preach the truth, and keep away from the ignorant ones."[110] In terms of forgiving insults, injuries, taunts, or criticism, the Prophet's (peace be upon him) patience was unequaled. He never inflicted pain or harm in return for pain and harm inflicted on him, except when God's cause was held up or God's laws were broken. Then and only then he took the appropriate action.

The people of Makkah[111] left no stone unturned in their desire to refute his claims and did all that was in their power to obstruct the laws of God. The Prophet (peace be upon him) was denied the right to worship God in his own way; he was severely insulted to the point that they spat on his face. On one occasion when the Prophet (peace be upon him) was preaching to the people of Al Taif,[112] he was roughly handled and showered with stones so that he bled profusely.

---

[107] The Quran. 2 (Surat Albaqara): 52. The story of Prophet Moses (peace be upon him), and the dividing of the Sea, and the worship of the calf.

[108] It was in Ghazwat Auhud (the battle of Auhud) this was the second battle for the Muslims with the Qurashis from Makkah.

[109] The Quran, 3 (Surat Al Imran): 155.

[110] The Quran, 7 (Surat Al'araf): 199.

[111] This was in early Islam, the first ten years of Mohamad's Prophecy (peace be upon him) to be precise. The majority of Makkans worshiped stones and idols, and then there was a well-established number of Jews and people who were on the belief of Prophet Abraham (peace be upon him), and fractional Christians.

[112] A mountain city, located 35-45 miles south of the city of Makkah, They are currently under the territorial jurisdiction of the Kingdom of Saudi Arabia.

In the midst of that situation he turned to God in prayer. However later when the Prophet triumphed over such people (e.g. when he triumphed over the people of Makkah and entered it [where he was tortured and suffered sorely during the early days of Islam there]), he forgave them and granted them full pardon.

He also suffered the same from his followers. They contributed to it by their rudeness and quick temper. In an occasion a Bedouin[113] man came and pulled Mohammed (peace be upon him) by his mantel until he almost fell down, and his neck turned red. The Bedouin said: "Mohammed! Give me from what God gave you".[114] Prophet Mohammed (peace be upon him) did not retaliate nor did he allow his friends, who rushed to put the man down. Instead the man was treated in well manner and given his need till pleased. Then the Bedouin man said: "O God! Forgive me, Mohammed and no one else". Mohammed (peace be upon him) explained to him that God's mercy is wide, and gracious and not limited to few and should not be limited in prayer.

In the previous examples the Prophet (peace be upon him) exemplified the Quran by commanding with forgiveness, and commanding justly what is right, and to stay away from the ignorant. "Have forgiveness, preach the truth, and keep away from the ignorant ones."[115] Mohammed's (peace be upon him) endurance is a living example of the Quranic descriptions of mercy and forgiveness. His reported conduct is Sunnah is a major part of Sharia law.

It is known that the Sharia Law wants to indoctrinate a genuine spirit of forgiveness and tolerance in the society. "(Muhammad), We have sent you for no other reason but to be a mercy for mankind."[116] But it must be known that the call and respect for the rule of law are equally respected. The Sharia confirms the need of criminal laws, particularly the Hodud. Humanity cannot turn one cheek after another, or forgive all the time, if it hurts the prospects of justice and serenity of the society. The offender in who all the means of

---

[113] Bedouins are people of the desert who lived in the desert in constant travel. Most of the Arabs were nomadic tribes that lived in constant travel for water and grazing grounds for their livestock.

[114] Referring to booty and money that the Muslims incurred in the expanding Muslim State.

[115] The Quran 7 (Al A'raf): 199.

[116] The Quran 21 (Al Anbiy'a): 107.

rehabilitative actions of compassion and forgiveness fail and is still determined to destabilize society and gears all his power to cause corruption on earth is to be treated with the same rigidity as the Hodud punishments are.

> The only proper recompense for those who fight against God and His messenger and try to spread evil in the land is to be killed, crucified, or either to have one of their hands and feet cut from the opposite side or to be sent into exile. These are to disgrace them in this life and they will suffer a great torment in the life hereafter.[117]

An example of that would be the criminals of the tribe of Urainah,[118] when they betrayed the people of Madinah (the people of Madinah treated the men from the tribe of Urainah with love and respect) by torturing and killing the herder of their camels and escaping with the camels as their booty. The Prophet (peace be upon him) quickly marshaled all his powers, arrested them, and dealt with them as prescribed in the Quranic verse for the Hudd of Hiraba because this was a matter of public interest that no were there could be room to forgive.

On the level of individuals, Muslims are given the right to seek judicial retribution, yet they are strongly encouraged in the virtue of forgiveness.

> The recompense for evil will be equivalent to the deed. He who pardons (the evil done to him) and reforms himself, will receive his reward from God. God certainly does not love the unjust.[119]

And in another verse:

> To exercise patience and forgive (the wrong done to one) is the proof of genuine determination.[120]

---

[117] The Quran, 5 (Surah Alma'iadah): 33.
[118] Urainah is an Arabian tribe.
[119] The Quran, 42 (Surat Alshura): 40.
[120] The Quran, 43 (Surat Alshura): 43.

God urges the Muslims to forgive. Muslims are strongly recommended to forgive and to forget bad feelings and open a new page.[121] Even in the most dreadful crime known to humanity, which is willful murder with full intent, God ordained Qisas (capital punishment) as an unquestionable right of Wali Aldam (the closest blood relative), which must be administered only if he insists upon it. But if his conscience is able to overcome fury and anguish and grant forgiveness, the death penalty is waived.

> Believers, in case of murder, the death penalty are the sanctioned retaliation: a free man for a free man, a slave for a slave, and a female for a female. However, if the convicted person receives pardon from the aggrieved party, the prescribed rules of compensation must be followed accordingly. This is a merciful alteration from your Lord. Whoever transgresses against it will face a painful punishment.[122]

In the Sunnah, the Prophet (peace be upon him) spared no effort in exhorting Muslims to adopt forgiveness in their conduct and adopt the concept of Sitr[123] for the protection of the reputation of others. This can be seen in the following three hadiths from the Sunnah:

> Whoever veils his Muslim brother's awrah,[124] God will veil his awrah in the hereafter. And whoever unveils the awrah of his brother Muslim, God will unveil his awrah even if he commits it in the most unseen part of his home.[125]

---

[121] The Quran, 64 (Surat Altghabun): 14.

[122] The Quran, 2 (Surat Albaqarah): 178.

[123] Sitr is the care to conceal and cover up in a humanitarian manner, the downfalls and negative side of others. A duty as not to cause defamation to others based on their negativities.

[124] Awrah is everything that if revealed about a person would be shamus to him/her. (e.g. If accidently a person's pants fell off in public and his private part were revealed.) The meaning of the word also extends to every action that could cause shame to the person if known to the public.

[125] Sunan Ibn Majah, "Kitab Alhodud", Vol. 2, p. 850.

Whoever protects the reputation of his brother by veiling his wrongful act, God will do the same to him in this world and the world to come.[126]

Whoever veils[127] a shameful act of a believer, is as if he resurrected a mawu'oudah[128]from her grave.[129]

The Sharia does not condone the crime, and forgiveness should never be interpreted to do such a thing because the community that is too ready to forgive may end up pardoning the crimes. It also must not be comprehended in a sense of inactiveness and virtue, as in "when struck on one cheek turn to be struck on the other."[130] Nor should it be considered as an effort or collaboration to harbor criminals as this is forbidden by Sharia and a major offence. It is the nature of the crime that allows clemency; the law also allows private action and clemency that involves any suitable settlement between the parties. It must be noted that forgiveness does not necessarily set the criminal free; the criminal may be required to restitutions, such as returning the stolen items or paying for it. (e.g. In the Hudd crime of Qathf, according to the Shafi'i school, a compensatory settlement is possible.) In crimes where the society in whole is a victim, such as drinking alcohol or Zina, the criminal can be subjected to reprimand and other means of reform.

Imam Malik, in regard to what was said previously, qualifies the forgiveness called for by the Prophet to be limited to first-time offenders as a means of rehabilitation. This gives them a chance to reconsider their

---

[126] Almustadrak "Kitab Alhodud", Vol. 4, p. 383.

[127] The word used in the hadith for veil was "Satara," from the word "Sitr".

[128] Mawu'ouda is the noun for the verb Wa'id. The Wai'id is on old pre-Islamic practice in the Arabic culture. They considered having a girl as a big shame, so they buried their baby girls alive. It is an awful and barbaric act that Islam banned. All Muslims regretted what they did before Islam, and almost most of them practiced that barbaric act. And after Islam they extremely regretted what they did and had this great regret and shame, which was a big burden. The Caliphate Omar did that before Islam, and after he converted to Islam he was known to cry whenever he remembered her until his beard dripped of tears because he remembered his baby girl wiping of the dust off his beard while he was burying her. This was the sense of Rahma and regret on the wrongdoings they did before Islam.

[129] Alsunan Alkubra, "Kitab Al Ashriba", Vol. 8, p. 331.

[130] Matthew 5:39 The Holy Bible

act and might heighten their compassion and concern to the wellbeing of others; it unwarps their minds to help them(the offenders) re-socialize. This is why I call it *Constructive Rehabilitative Forgiveness* (CRF), a term I personally coined, because Islamic law (Sharia law) calls for CRF, which is using forgiveness as a rehabilitative act for the offender and constructive for the community to promote higher moral standard.[131] If the criminal was found to be serial in his actions, repeatedly committing the crimes and offenses, he is to be handed over to the authorities. Likewise, if an offender is forgiven but misjudges forgiveness (looks at forgiveness as a mean of getting away with it, and next time he won't get caught) and repeats the offence, it becomes unavoidable on the people and society to subject him to the legal process and its harsh consequences. Such an offender after exhausting the means of CRF would need physical deterrence. In the Hudod we find the means of rigidity and sternness required for such punishment, and others would find sufficient deterrence.[132]

All the Hudod crimes, legally speaking, are according to the Sunnah previously cited in this section and are susceptible to forgiveness. The Sunnah specifies the Hudod to be subject to clemency and forgiveness, but its extension to other crimes is strictly subject to legal possibility

I must note that the forgiveness of a Hudd crime requires that it take place before the case is reported officially to the authorities. The

---

[131] This is also what I call the Saudi Monasaha program (Prince Mohammed Bin Naif's program for terrorist rehabilitation) CRF. CRF is an old concept that has been newly born through the Monasha program that Prince Naif bin Abdulaziz established. In modern communities where the ties between communities are severed, the only way to promote such constructive rehabilitation is through programs that promote forgiveness. I remember during a lecture by Professor Mark Shulman at Pace University during the fall semester of 2011, we were asked if there would be a devise that would convict and judge people accurately with one hundred percent efficiency. There was a debate on that question. The truth about that question is if we truly had such efficiency we would probably not have compassion and clemency, which are values important for the development of humanity. And law would be more vindictive; I believe that the purpose of Laws and legislation is to promote a better community to live in. Without forgiveness and moral values we would not have a healthy community to live in; a lot of things in the world in essence is legal yet not moral.

[132] This was an elaboration of Malik's view in his book Almudawanah Alkubra (The great encyclopedia) Vol. 4, p. 415.

Islamic jurists (four major Islamic schools) are unanimous in that once a case is officially reported, forgiveness is not permitted. Malik defines "authorities" as including guardsmen and police. In his opinion, if the offender is caught by or is reported to them, no forgiveness is possible.[133]

In conclusion, the concept of forgiveness is effective in Islamic communities that have been in practicing Sharia for a long time. (e.g. In the middle east Islamic law existed, and the region has been ruled in the same concept for more than 1400 years, and the people have the ideology that helps them accept this concept.) Today, in a multicultural city it could not be imagined, but it is not impossible. It could be present in certain sections of cities or villages, where people maintain good neighborly relations and know each other. If an inhabitant of such closely related communities commits a Hudd, forgiveness is imaginable, and then forgiveness can perform its constructive rehabilitative purpose to further strengthen the ties of the community.

Forgiveness is optional and dependable on circumstances conducive to its benefit. There is no obligation to forgive, but it is preferable and Sharia law urges it and tolerates it. The last thing is that I do not know where forgiveness is applicable in the modern separation of powers theory. In the Sunnah, the Prophet's (peace be upon him) conduct was based on his powers as a judge. He would not forgive the Hudod if it reached him, yet urged people to forgive before it reached him as a judge. Can we imagine with the modern separation of powers that the administrative side of the government has a certain role to forgive? Especially when there is a case not officially reported. I imagine it to be that way in some sense; such a hypothesis would need further research.

Intercession "Shafa'ah"[134]

Intercession is an act of mediating on behalf of the offender for forgiveness. The mediator can do it voluntarily or by request of the offender or a third party. Intercession is a means of further pursuance of

---

[133] Almudawanah Alkubra, Vol. 4, p. 287.

[134] Shafa'ah is the Arabic word for intercession. Whice is an act of pleading on behalf the offender for clemency and forgiveness.

the objective of Rahma (forgiveness/clemency). The Prophet urged Muslims to intercede in the following hadith: "Intercede for forgiveness before the Hudd reaches the person in charge."[135] In the light of the hadith, I would like to elaborate with the story of Alzubair bin Alawwam, a companion of the Prophet (peace be upon him). Alzubair met some people escorting a thief to the authorities, and he interceded for forgiveness. The people promised to forgive, but after taking him to the judge, Alzubair then said: "No! If it reaches the judge, then God curses the intercessor and the one who would grant intercession."[136]

Similar to forgiveness, in intercession once the case is reported to the authorities, mediation is banned. At this stage, meaning after reaching the authorities, intercession would be considered obstruction of justice or a cause of segregation in handing down verdicts or their administration. Therefore, the Prophet (peace be upon him) cautioned against it in the following hadith: "The one whose intercession has prevented an implementation of a Hudd, has actually outraged God's command."[137]

The Sunnah sources have unanimously reported the Prophet's (peace be upon him) resentment of his closest companion Osamah bin Zaid's intercession to prevent the application of the Sarika Hudd against an honorable woman from Bani Makhzoum.[138] They asked Osamah to plead on their behalf. They even offered a considerable amount of gold as compensation for the women's theft. The Prophet (peace be upon him) conveyed anguish on Osamah's intervention to mediate, and addressed the audience condemning any inequality before the law or any intercession that could cause discrimination. The Prophet (peace be upon him) vowed that even if his daughter Fatima stole, he would cut her hand off without reluctance.[139] Prophet Mohammed (peace be upon him) was also angry when some Muslims covered up for a fellow tribesman who intruded into another man's property in a try to mislead the Prophet (peace be upon him) into charging a Jewish man until the truth came to him through the Quranic verse:

---

[135] Sunan Abi Dawod "Kitab Alhoudu", Vol. 4, p. 383.

[136] Almuwata', "Kitab Alhudod", Vol. 2, p. 835.

[137] Almustadrak, "Kitab Alhudod", Vol. 4, p. 383.

[138] A well-known Arabian tribe; the woman was from that tribe. The woman was considered to be from an honorable branch of the tribe, a daughter of a sheikh.

[139] Sahih Albukhari, "Bab Hadith Alghar", Vol. 4, p. 151.

We have revealed to you the Book in all the Truth so that you judge among people by the laws of God. However, never defend the treacherous ones.[140]

Therefore the Prophet (peace be upon him) made a clear line as to when forgiveness and intercession are desirable and when they are considered detrimental to the cause of justice. The Quran and the Prophet's (peace be upon him) Sunnah ban apartheid in the legal system; all people are equal under Sharia. Upholding the rule of law and preserving everlasting respect for it are supreme goals of the Sharia.

No Pleasure in Seeing the Hudd:

The day a Hudd punishment is applied is a sad day for all Muslims. The Prophet (peace be upon him), particularly to first time offenders, felt sadness and sorrow when he saw the actual infliction of the Hudd punishment (e.g. the reported case through Abdullah bin Masu'ud in his memories of the first man ever to have his hand amputated for theft and the excessive paleness of the Prophet's [peace upon him] face that was caused by his severe sadness). While in that condition, his companions asked him if he didn't like what was happening. Prophet Mohammed (peace be upon him) replied:

> And what forbids me from being so? Do not be the supporters of the devil on your brother. It is not for me as a Ruler to forgive a Hudd after it has reached me. But you should remember that God is forgiving and he likes

---

[140] The Quran, 4 (Surat Alnisa'): 105

The case that the prophet was faced with was the case of Taymah ibn Ubayraq, who was a hypocrite, only nominally a Muslim. Taymah stole and armor, and when the trail was hot, Taymah planted the stolen goods in the house of a Jew in Madinah, where it was eventually found. The Jewish man denied the charge and accused Taymah, but the Muslims felt sympathy towards Taymah (nominally Muslim). The case reached the Prophet, who acquitted the Jewish man according to the strict principles of Justice in Sharia. As attempts were made to deceive the Prophet into favoring Taymah, and when Taymah realized deceiving didn't work and they wouldn't favor a Muslim over Jew and his punishment was imminent, he ran away and turned apostate.

forgiveness. Do not you read: "Be considerate and forgiving. Do you not want God to forgive you? God is All-forgiving and Al-merciful."[141]

Another incident of not having pleasure in administering the Hudod punishment was the Prophet's (peace be upon him) attempts to stop Ma'az from making his confession to the Hudd of Zina. The Prophet (peace be upon him) repelled him countless times until he disappeared from site then came back.[142] In some other reports of the case he turned him back three times,[143] and the Hudd was applied only when Ma'az was persistent and did not yield. It was reported that Ma'az, before going to the Prophet (peace be upon him), consulted his trusted friend Huthal. His friend advised him to confess to the Prophet (peace be upon him). After Ma'az was stoned to death, the Prophet Mohammed (peace be upon him) addressed Huthal with the following: "Oh, Huthal! If you had veiled him with your mantel it would have been better for you."[144] (As to the advice that Huthal gave Ma'az was not right he should have veiled ["Satarhu" from the word "Sitr"] him and told him to go back to God and conceal it and regret what he did.)

In fact, when Ma'az felt the pain of being stoned, he tried to escape but was caught, and the stoning continued. When knowledge of that reached the Prophet, he talked to the executors of the Hudd saying: "You could have let him go. He might have repented and God would have forgiven him."[145]

The Prophet's (peace be upon him) conduct was in the same manner with a woman from the tribe of Ghamid.[146] She confessed and he tried to urge her to self-remorse, but she insisted to be purified

---

[141] Almustadrak, "Kitab Alhudod", Vol. 4, pp. 381–384. The Prophet referred to the Quran in the hadith (Quran24: 22)

[142] Almubasat, Vol. 9, p. 92.

[143] Sahih Muslim "Kitabd Alhudod", Vol. 3, p. 1322.

[144] Amuwata' "Kitab Alhodud", Vol. 3, p. 1322. The meaning of the hadith, to veil with the mantil, is if you have advised him to not come and repent and told him that god was forgiving. And Sitr by covering up his sin.

[145] Sunan Altirmithi, "Kitab Alhodud", Vol. 4, pp. 27–29.

[146] Ghamid is an Arabic tribe with a known territorial coverage in the western region and southern western region of the Arabian Peninsula, mostly in Tihamat Aseer. Now most of the tribe is in the territorial jurisdiction of the Kingdom of Saudi Arabia.

by the punishment. She was pregnant and was allowed to deliver then given enough time to breast feed the child and wean her child before she was stoned to death.

There is no doubt now that Sharia law is not vindictive. We notice that there is nothing ritual or of religious pleasure in witnessing the Hudd punishment applied. In fact, Hudd punishments are a last resort measure. Such punishments are also important for an effective justice system that promotes tranquility and a well-disciplined society. The Prophet strongly advised people to settle the cases of Hudod among themselves. Even if a Hudd reached the courts and a trial is initiated, the existence of any Shubha (doubt), as particularly emphasized by the Sunnah, shall bar the application of the Hudd punishment. Nevertheless, the Prophet's (peace be upon him) attitude should never be construed as minimizing the constitutional supremacy of the Hudod in a Sharia legal system. If all the requirements for the Hudd are satisfied judicially, the Hudd must be implemented as prescribed without any wavering.

Mercy in the Current Islamic Legal System and How to Implement It in other Legal Systems

"Do not let the hostility of a group of people keep you away from the Sacred Mosque or make you express animosity. Co-operate with each other in righteousness and piety, not in sin and hostility. Have fear of God; he is stern in His retribution."[147] In this verse Muslims have been ordered to be righteous and help to contribute to and enforce high moral standards in the community and cooperate to reach social harmony. One of the applications of mercy/clemency in current Islamic legal system is His Royal Highness Prince Mohammed bin Naif's rehabilitation program for terrorists and Guantanamo Bay detainees. The program is targeted to persuade Muslim Jihadi extremists to abandon the policy of violence that they have adopted. This program is not an imprisonment program, but one intended to rehabilitate, helping its participants to comprehend where they went wrong and how to avoid plummeting back into the same activities/patterns that trapped them in the first place.[148] On June 2011, the number of people that benefited from the program has been reported to be more than four hundred rehabilitees.[149]

---

[147] The Quran, 5 (Alma'ida): 2.

[148] http://xrdarabia.org/2009/01/26/saudi-terrorist-rehab-program-still-works/ last visited 3/14/2012. The article says that 218 were submitted into the program. Two hundred fourteen reformed, and four people returned to their deviated ideological thoughts and back to the spiral of crime.

[149] http://www.aawsat.com/details.asp?section=4andissueno=11873andarticle=624516a ndfeature=. Last visited on 3/16/2012. The Middle East Newspaper reported the introduction of twenty-two rehabilitees into the community, and further on elaborated that the number of people who benefited from the program has reached four hundred reformed terrorists, to the date of the article on June of 2011.

After a wave of devastating terrorist attacks on the Kingdom of Saudi Arabia in 2003, Saudi Arabia has launched an extensive campaign to combat terrorism. The use of non-conventional measures (soft methods, forgiveness, and clemency) aimed at combating intellectual and ideological justifications for extremism was a major aspect of Saudi efforts. The main objective of this strategy is to fight the extremists' ideology that is based on a corrupt and perverted interpretation of Islam. The Saudi government recognizes that it cannot fight against violent extremism through traditional security measures alone.[150] Thus they adopted CRF (Constructive Rehabilitative Forgiveness) methods of rehabilitation in Prince Mohammed's rehabilitative program.

The best way to shed light on this method is Khalid Aljihani's story. Khalid was released from Guantanamo Bay, and a Saudi 747 plane was dispatched to pick him up and return him to Saudi Arabia. (This process has been done with all the Guantanamo Bay releases.) Aljihani was one of Bin Laden's disciples. Aljihani elaborated on that when he said, "I've been involved in this jihad thing since I was young. I believed that I have to help the Muslims and this is the right way to do it—to perform jihad." Aljihani went to Afghanistan in the '90s and was with Bin Laden in Tora Bora in the course of al Qaeda's last stand against the Americans. The last stand in Tora Bora left Aljihani with an entirely different opinion of Bin Laden. Aljihani explains about his experience with Bin Laden: "He said 'Well, I'm not going to let you down and you are not going to let us down.' But I saw that in Tora Bora that when he left, so he left everybody behind him, you know." After spending four years in Guantanamo Bay then enrolling into the CRF program back in Saudi Arabia, he became a primary example of how the Saudi government treats one-time holy warriors it no longer considers a threat. After he finished the program and was back into the society for one month, he said: "After one month they call me and said 'Ok—go on, get your car.' I said car? Okay." He continued to say, "All the people that have been released from Guantanamo, they give them car to you know, to help them get in the society." The CRF program did not stop at that; it also paid for his marriage and house and fully introduced him into the society as a new man with a family. The CRF program aims to give

---

[150] http://www.assakina.com/center/files/5307.html. Last visited 3/17/2012.

them a new life in which they prosper and not go back to the deviated ideology that previously ruined their lives.[151]

Another story is Al Awfi's story, which was one of the stories that wasn't a total success. Awfi came back from six years in Guantanamo in a back brace, went through rehabilitation, but then swapped the back brace for a bandolier. And along with another ex-student of the CRF program showed up in Yemen on an al Qaeda video denouncing the Saudi government. He was back on the Saudi terrorist list then returned to hand himself to the Saudi authorities. "He ran away. And now he's back and he gets to see his wife every day. He has to be the only ex-terrorist in the world that is living in an apartment with the permission of his government."[152] The Saudi government still dealt with him with the Islamic Rahma concept because he surrendered. The silver lining to this story is that he still handed himself in.*id*

In conclusion, I truly believe in the Islamic concept of CRF and in the current Saudi CRF program for reforming terrorists and Guantanamo Bay detainees. I have great admiration for the program and would like to point out and thank H.R.H Crowned Prince Naif Bin Abdulaziz, Deputy Premier and Minister of Interior, for his support for this program. I would love to see this program continue and expand to cover rehabilitation, which does not only apply for terrorists and former Guantanamo detainees. In my opinion the Western legal systems can benefit from adopting the Saudi CRF program as well. Criticism to the Saudi CRF program is based on a less than ten percent failure rate; the Saudi CRF has a success rate of ninety percent, which is well above average in comparison to any other known rehabilitative programs. "Saudi authorities claim a rehabilitation success rate of 80 to 90 percent, having re-arrested only 35 individuals for security offenses."[153]

---

[151] http://forums.islamicawakening.com/f18/reeducating-osama-bin-ladens-disciples-24351/. The whole story of Khalid Aljihani was from the website, same as the quotes. All of the paragraphs related to the story have been heavily based on the article.

[152] http://forums.islamicawakening.com/f18/reeducating-osama-bin-ladens-disciples-24351/. Last visited on 3/16/2012. Al Awfi's story and the paragraphs related to the story have been based on the article.

[153] http://www.carnegieendowment.org/2008/09/22/saudi-arabia-s-soft-counterterrorism-strategy-prevention-rehabilitation-and-aftercare/s4. Last visited 5/16/2012 5:00 p.m. I have also visited the CBS news website, and viewed *60 Minutes* in a program related to the topic. http://www.cbsnews.com/video/watch/?id=4988100n. I have been influenced by *60 Minutes* in my writings about the rehabilitation program.

Conclusion

In conclusion, regarding forgiveness in Sharia law (Where the Quran and Sunnah are the constitution), I would like to point out the following:

1- That the application of the concepts of forgiveness is a constitutional matter and must be applied through the paths that were set in the Sharia itself.

2- In Sharia law there is equity and equality in courts. This constitutes that under the law all the people are treated equally.

3- Sharia law does not look at the application of the harsh punishments of the Hudod as a religious ritual; it strongly urges new findings and the development of legal technicalities (e.g. giving the person the benefit of the doubt, or certain ways for evidential enquiries and acquisition).

4- The burden of proof in some Hudd crimes is very complicated to the point of technical impossibility of application, and the only means of proof would be a willing confession. In fact not just willing, more like insisting on confessing.

There surely is a concept and underlying custom and norm for the application of Rahma (clemency) in the Hudod as long as it is not in front of a judge. An important point that I saved for last in my paper—that there is a prophetic hadith of considerable weight of authority that Ibn Abbas reported—the Prophet (peace be upon him) said:

"Neither the slave nor the People of the Book are liable for hudod."[154] Ibn Abbas concurs and supports the previous hadith.

---

[154] Sunan Aldaraqutni, "Kitab Alhodud wa Aldiyat" Vol. 3, p. 87. The people of the book in the hadith are the Jews and Christians.

According to the previous hadith—if accepted by the majority—the Hudod only apply on Muslims. I strongly request that the Islamic scholars of hadith investigate this hadith and inform the Islamic community on the authority of this hadith.

Bibliography

1- [1] Abu Abdullah Mohammed Ahmed Alansari Al Qurtubi, Aljami' li ahkam al Quran (RiyadhL Maktabat Al Riyadh al Hadithah, 1952).

2- Abdelqadir Alshaybani, Nayl Almatalib Be Sharh Dalil Altalib (Kuwait: Maktabat Al Falah, 1983).

3- Abdulhakim Altahawi, Al Malik Faisal Wa al Alaqat al Kharigiyah al Saudia [King Faisal and the Saudi Foreign Relation] 34–54 (2002).

4- Abu Lubaba. Altarbiya fil alsunnah alnabawiya (Education in the prophetic Sunnah). Riyahd: Dar alliwa'a 1977. (This book talks about the prophets discipline and way of education) will help with the research.

5- Ahmed H. Dahlaan, Dirasa Fi al Siyasah al Dakhiliyah Li Al Mamlakah al Arabia al Saudia [Study in the Internal Politics of the Kingdom of Saudi Arabia] (1984).

6- Ahmed H. Dahlan, The Saudi Arabian Council of Ministers: its Environment, its Role and its Future, in Politics, Administration and Development in Saudi Arabia 66–67 (Ahmed H. Dahlan ed., 1990).

7- Al Dur Almukhtar Sharh Tanweer Al Absar, Published with Ibn Abdeen, Hashiat Radd Almuhtar (Egypt: Dar Alfikr, 1979).

8- Al'a Aldeen Kasani, Badai' Alsanai' (Beirut: Dar Alkatib Al arabi, 1982).

9- Alaffani. Aljaza'a mn jin al amal (Be the penalty be the deed). Cairo: the Library of Ibn taymiya 1996. (This book mostly talks about penalties based on Islamic theories and gives examples.)

10- Albukhari. Sahih Albukhari. Dar tog alnajat 1422 (Islamic calendar). (Bukhari is an affirmative source and very strong source of Sunnah according to all of Islamic scholars [Shia'a and Sunnah].)

11- Ali Alkattani. Resurgence of Islam in Andalusia. Lebanon: Dar Alkutub al ilmiya, 2005. (This is a historical study about the society of Andalusia, now known as the State of Spain and Portugal.)

12- Bahnasi. Altazeer fil islam (Non hodud Punishment in Islam). Cairo: Alkhaleej al arabi 1988. (This book talks about Islamic law in the case of Tazeer non hodudic punishments.)

13- Dr. Adel Abduljabar. Al irhab fe mizan alshariya (Terrorism in the view of Islamic law). (This book talks about terrorism and the required action in accordance to Islamic law.)

14- Dr. Akram Alomary. Almujtama'a al madani. Library of the Islamic university in Madina. (The community of the city of Madina during the era of the Prophet. The talk mainly talks about the early Islamic community rules and regulations. And it also sheds some light on the constitution of Madina, which was written to regulate interaction with the Jewish minority in Madina.)

15- Dr. Raghib Alsirhany. http://www.islamstory.com/-الرحمة-في-حياة-رسول-الله. 4/12/2010. (This article is about mercy and its application through the life of the prophet.)

16- Dr. Raghib Alsirhany. http://www.islamstory.com/-تعامل-رسول-الله-مع-الأقليات-غير-المسلمة-بالمدينة. 4/28/2010. (How the Prophet organized and regulated the non-Muslim minorities in Madina.)

17- Dr. Raghib Alsirhany. http://www.islamstory.com/-رسول-الله-وحقوق-الحيوان. 4/27/2010. (Mercy and animal rights in Islam. This fact has been neglected in our current legal system and should be applied.)

18- Dr. Raghib Alsirjany. http://www.islamstory.com/-أخلاق ر سول-الله-مع-الأسرى .4/28/2011. (The way the Prophet treated prisoners of war.)

19- Dr. Raghib Alsirjany. http://www.islamstory.com/-الجمال الانساني-في-حسن-الخلق .5/17/2010. (Mostly about social conduct in Islam.)

20- Dr. Raghib Alsirjany. http://www.islamstory.com/-الرحمة-في الإسلام-أهميتها-ونماذج-منها .5/12/2010. (Mercy in Islam application and importance.)

21- Dr. Raghib Alsirjany. http://www.islamstory.com/-القتال-في الاسلام-راغب-السرجاني .12/25/2011. (War in Islam.)

22- Dr. Raghib Alsirjany. http://www.islamstory.com/-رحمة للعالمين-الرحمة-المهداة .12/6/2011. (Talks about how Islam promotes international peace.)

23- Dr. Raghib Alsirjany. http://www.islamstory.com/-عفو الرسول .6/12/2011. (The leniency and mercy of the Prophet.)

24- Dr. Raghib Alsirjany. http://www.islamstory.com/-من مميزات-الحضارة-الاسلامية .1/30/2012. (The positive features of the Islamic civilization.)

25- Dr. Yousef alkharadawi. Fikh al awlawiyat. www.fiseb.com. (This book I do not like much but talks about hodud, amd general fikh.)

26-   Dr.Raghib alsirhany.
http://www.islamstory.com/%D8%AA%D8%B7%D8%A8%D
9%8A%D9%82-
%D8%A7%D9%84%D8%B4%D8%B1%D9%8A%D8%B9%
D8%A9. 6/13/2011. (Talks about the application of Hodud,
how it applies—when and how.)

27-   Edwar Ghali, Mu'amalat ghair almuslimeen fil mujtama'a al
islami (treatment of non-Muslims in a Muslim community).
Library of Ghareeb, 1993.

28-   Faisal bin Mishal, Islamic Political Development in the
Kingdom of Saudi Arabia; Majlis Al Shura: Concept, Theory
and Practice (2002).

29-   Friday Prayer Khotba in the Prophet's Mosque in Madinah by
Shaikh Alhothayfi 8/17/1422 (Islamic calendar). (This sheikh
talks about Hodud and mercy in the lecture that is before the
weekly Friday prayer.)

30-   http://ikhwanwayonline.wordpress.com/2012/01/19/%D8%AF
%D8%B1%D8%A1-
%D8%A7%D9%84%D8%AD%D8%AF%D9%88%D8%AF-
%D8%A8%D8%A7%D9%84%D8%B4%D8%A8%D9%87%
D8%A7%D8%AA-
%D9%82%D8%B1%D8%A7%D8%A1%D8%A9-
%D9%81%D9%89-
%D9%85%D9%88%D8%B3%D9%88%D8%B9%D8%A9-
%D8%A7%D9%84/. 1/19/2012, 7:14 PM. (About how not to
apply Hodud, and theories of shubha to not apply the Hodud.)

31-   http://islamqa.info/ar/ref/9935. Last visited 3/15/2012 at 6:00
p.m.

32-   http://www.aawsat.com/details.asp?section=4andissueno=1187
3andarticle=624516andfeature=.

33-   http://www.assakina.com/center/files/5307.html.

34-   http://www.bt.com.bn/files/digital/Islamia/Issue101/SP4Jun.4.pdf.

35-   http://www.hanialtanbour.com/maw/30/source/01/book041.htm.

36-   http://www.jameataleman.org/agas/tasher/tasher10.htm.
       (General talk about strict application of Hodud.)

37-   http://www.shura.gov.sa/wps/wcm/connect/ShuraEn/internet/F
       istorical+BG. Last visited March 3, 2012.

38-   http://www.sudanradio.info/php/vb.353/archive/index.php/t-
       7471.html. 2008 2:50 p.m. (Has a few interesting hadiths, and
       talks about a case of the drinking haad from Hodud.)

39-   http://www.yanabi.com/Hadith.aspx?HadithID=13914.

40-   http://xrdarabia.org/2009/01/26/saudi-terrorist-rehab-program-
       still-works/.

41-   Ibn Othaymeen.
       http://www.ibnothaimeen.com/all/books/article_18174.shtml
       . 4/15/2007. (Talks about Sitr in Islam, a great article by
       Shaikh Ibn Othaymeen.)

42-   Mansour Al Bahuti, Kashshaf Alqina' 'an matn Aliqna'
       (Beirut: Dar al Fikr, 1982).

43-   Mohammed Ahmad Al Rakbi, Alnathm Almusdhdhab Fi Sharh
       Gharib Almuhathab, Published with Abi Ishaq Al Shirazi,
       Almuhadhdhab, (Egypt Dar Ihya Al kutub Al' Arabia).

44-   Muslim Bin Hajaj. Sahih Muslim. Dar ihya'a alturath alarabi-
       Beirut. (This is also a source of Sunnah exactly as strong a
       Bukhari.)

45-   Musnad Abu Hanifah "Musnad Ikrimah wa Muqsim."

46-   Quranic translation by Ibn Katheer.

47-   Sharaf aldin al maqdasi, Al iqna' (Beirut: Dar al Ma'rifah n.d).

48-   Soliman A. Sulaim, Constitutional and Judicial Organization in
       Saudi Arabia (1970).

49-   Sunan Altirmithi. (Islamic Sunnah source).

50-   The Basic Law of Governance (Saudi constitution articles).

51-   The Custodian of the holy mosques' Fahd bin Abdulaziz,
       Speech on the Issuance of the Basic Law of Governance (Mar.
       11, 1992).

52- The Holy Quran.

53- The Sunnah.

54- Zaidan. Alsunan al ilhiya (The Devine will). Mu'asasat alrisala. (about the devine will, and interpertaions, and multiple topics).

55- Zain Al Din Ibn Nujaim, Albahr Al Raiq Sharh Kanz Al daqauq (Pakistan: Al Mutba'ah Al'Arabiyya n.d).

56- http://theamericanmuslim.org/tam.php/features/articles/fatwa_f reedom_of_belief_minority_rights_in_muslim_countries.

57- http://www.passia.org/meetings/rsunit/Islamic-Schools-Jurisprudence.htm.

58- http://www.carnegieendowment.org/2008/09/22/saudi-arabia-s-soft-counterterrorism-strategy-prevention-rehabilitation-and-aftercare/s4.

59- http://ibrahimlong.com/2010/04/29/41/.

Glossary

1- Alhiraba: organized crime such as highway robbery, and terrorism.

2- Almuhsan: a person who has had intercourse within a valid marriage.

3- Altaif: Ta'if (Arabic الطائف aṭ-Ṭā'if) is a city in the Mecca Province of Saudi Arabia at an elevation of 1,879 m (6,165 ft) on the slopes of the Sarawat Mountains (Al-Sarawat Mountains). It has a population of 521,273 (2004 census). Each summer the Saudi Government moves from the heat of Riyadh to Ta'if. The city is the Centre of an agricultural area known for its grapes, roses, and honey.

4- Awrah: Parts of the body that are not supposed to be exposed to others.

5- Ayah: Ayah or Aayah (Arabic: آية āyah, plural: ayat or ayaat آيات āyāt) is the Arabic word for evidence or sign: "These are the Ayat (proofs, evidences, verses, lessons, revelations, etc.) of Allah, which We recite to you (O Muhammad SAW) with truth. Then in which speech after Allah and His Ayat will they believe?" (Surat Al-Jathiya 45:6, Mohsin Khan translation of the Qur'an) The word is usually used to refer to the smallest unit of the Qur'an, usually called "verses" or "signs" in English translations of the Qur'an. Muslims believe that each ayah of the Qur'an is a sign from God. Chapters in the Qur'an, called suras in Arabic, are made up of several ayat, although suras vary greatly in length, ranging from 3 to 286 ayat. Within a long sura, ayat may be further divided into thematic sequences or passages. A common myth persists that the number of ayat in the Qur'an is 6,666. In fact, the total number of ayat in all suras is 6,236; the number varies if the bismillahs are counted separately. The verse number is written in a symbol at the end of each verse. This symbol is ⬤, end of ayah. Its Unicode number is U+06DD. The word ayah is also used to refer to the verses of the Bible by Arab Christians and Christians in countries where Arabic words are used for religious term.

6-   Ayat: is the plural of Ayah.

7-   Caliphate Ali: Alī ibn Abī Ṭālib (Arabic: علي بن أبي طالب؛ Ali was also the cousin and son-in-law of the Islamic prophet Muhammad and ruled over the Islamic Caliphate from 656 to 661. He was the first male convert to Islam. Sunnis consider Ali the fourth and final of the Rashidun (rightly guided Caliphs). Ali migrated to Medina shortly after Muhammad did. Once there Muhammad told Ali that God had ordered Muhammad to give his daughter, Fatimah, to Ali in marriage. For the ten years that Muhammad led the community in Medina, Ali was extremely active in his service, leading parties of warriors on battles and carrying messages and orders. Ali took part in the early caravan raids from Mecca and later in almost all the battles fought by the nascent Muslim community. Ali was appointed Caliph by the Companions of Muhammad (the Sahaba) in Medina after the assassination of the third caliph, Othman ibn Affan. He encountered defiance and civil war during his reign. In 661, Ali was attacked one morning while worshipping in the mosque of Kufa and died a few days later. Ali is respected for his courage, knowledge, belief, honesty, unbending devotion to Islam, deep loyalty to Muhammad, equal treatment of all Muslims, and generosity in forgiving his defeated enemies. Ali retains his stature as an authority on Quranic exegesis, Islamic jurisprudence, and religious thought.

8-   Caliphate Omar: ⬚Umar ibn al-Khaṭṭāb (Arabic عمر بن الخطاب), c. 586–590 –644c. 2 November (Dhu al-Hijjah 26, 23 Hijri[2]), was a leading companion and adviser to the Islamic prophet Muhammad who later became the second Muslim

Caliph after Muhammad's death. Converting to Islam in the sixth year after Muhammad's first revelation, he spent seventeen years as a companion of Muhammad. He succeeded Caliph Abu Bakr on 23 August 634, and played a significant role in Islamic history. Under his rule the Islamic empire expanded at an unprecedented rate, conquering the whole territory of the former Sassanid Empire and more than two thirds of the Byzantine Empire. His legislative abilities, his firm political and administrative control over a rapidly expanding empire, and his brilliantly coordinated attacks against the Sassanid Persian Empire that resulted in the conquest of the Persian Empire in less than two years marked his reputation as a great political and military leader. He was assassinated by a Persian captive. Sunni Muslims view him as the Second Rightly-Guided Caliph and know him as al-Farooq (he who knows truth from falsehood).

9- Caliphate: The term caliphate, "dominion of a caliph ('successor')" (from the Arabic خلافة or khilāfa, Turkish: Hilafet), refers to the first system of government established in Islam and represented the political unity of the Muslim Ummah (community). In theory, it is an aristocratic–constitutional republic (the Constitution being the Constitution of Medina), which means that the head of state, the Caliph, and other officials are representatives of the people and of Islam and must govern according to constitutional and religious law, or Sharia. In its early days, it resembled elements of direct democracy (see shura) and an elective monarchy. It was initially led by Muhammad's disciples as a continuation of the political and religious system the prophet established, known as the "Rashidun caliphates." A *caliphate* is also a state that implements such a governmental system. Sunni Islam stipulates that the head of state, the caliph, should be selected by Shura— elected by Muslims or their representatives.

10- CRF (Constructive Rehabilitative Forgiveness): This is a term I use to describe the Saudi rehabilitative program to reform terrorist/Guantanamo Bay detainees because the program is innovative, and it's truly Islamic in nature and application. It depends on applying the concepts of Rahma/Sitr. It uses forgiveness and generosity as rehabilitative tools, and has showed a ninety percent success rate.

11- Ghair Almuhsan: a person who has not had intercourse with in a valid marriage.

12- Hudd: A boundary or limit. A statutory punishment defined by Sharia law. It is the singular of Hudod.

13- Hijaz Region: al-Hejaz, also Hijaz (Arabic: الحجاز al-Ḥiǧāz, literally "the barrier") is a region in the west of present-day Saudi Arabia. Defined primarily by its western border on the Red Sea. It extends from Haql on the Gulf of Aqaba to Jizan. Its main city is Jeddah, but it is probably better known for the Islamic holy cities of Mecca and Medina. As the site of Islam's holy places, the Hejaz has significance in the Arab and Islamic historical and political landscape. The region is so called as it separates the land of Najd in the east from the land of Tihamah in the west.

14- Hirz: A well-secured place. When a thing is in safekeeping, it is in a Hirz. When something is in a Hirz, it is to be Mahrooz.

15- Hudod: Hudud (Arabic, also transliterated Hadud, Hudod; singular Hudd or Hadd, حد, literal meaning "limit", or "restriction") is the word often used in Islamic literature for the bounds of acceptable behavior and the punishments for serious crimes. In Islamic law or Sharia, Hudud usually refers to the class of punishments that are fixed for certain crimes that are considered to be "claims of God." They include theft, fornication and adultery (Zina), consumption of alcohol or other intoxicants (Khamr), and apostasy (see apostasy in Islam).

16- Huquq Lilahi Ta'ala: It means it is a right of God, belonging to God.

17- King Abdulaziz: King Abdul-Aziz of Saudi Arabia (1876–9 November 1953) (Arabic: عبد العزيز آل سعود, 'Abd al-'Azīz Āl Su'ūd) was the first monarch of Saudi Arabia, the third Saudi State. He was usually called Ibn Saud in English-speaking countries. Beginning with the re-conquest of his family's ancestral home city of Riyadh in 1902, he consolidated his control over the Najd in 1922 then conquered the Hijaz in 1925. Having conquered almost all of central Arabia, he united his dominions into the Kingdom of Saudi Arabia in 1932. As King, he presided over the discovery of petroleum in Saudi Arabia in 1938 and the beginning of large-scale oil exploitation after World War II. He was the father of many children, including all of the subsequent kings of Saudi Arabia

18- King Fahd: Fahd bin Abdul Aziz Al Saud, Custodian of the Two Holy Mosques, (Arabic: فهد بن عبد العزيز آل سعود Fahd ibn 'Abd al-'Azīz Āl Su'ūd) (16 March 1921– August 2005) was King of Saudi Arabia from 1982 to 2005. One of forty-five sons of Saudi founder Ibn Saud, and the fourth of his five sons who have ruled the Kingdom (Saud, Faisal, Khalid, Fahd, and Abdullah), Fahd ascended to the throne on the death of his half-brother, King Khalid, on 13 June 1982. Fahd was appointed Crown Prince when Khalid succeeded their half-brother King Faisal, who was assassinated in 1975. Fahd was viewed as the de facto prime minister during King Khalid's reign in part due to the latter's ill health. Fahd suffered a debilitating stroke on 29 November 1995, after which he was unable to continue performing his full official duties. His half-brother, Abdullah, the country's Crown Prince, served as de facto regent of the kingdom and succeeded Fahd as monarch upon his death on 1 August 2005. King Fahd is credited for having introduced the Basic Law of Saudi Arabia in 1992.

19- King Faisal: Faisal bin Abdul-Aziz Al Saud (1906–March 25, 1975) (Arabic: فيصل بن عبدالعزيز آل سعود Fayṣal ibn 'Abd al-'Azīz Āl Su'ūd) was King of Saudi Arabia from 1964 to 1975. As king, he is credited with rescuing the country's finances and implementing a policy of modernization and reform, while his main foreign policy themes were pan-Islamism, anti-Communism, and pro-Palestinian nationalism. He successfully stabilized the kingdom's bureaucracy and his reign had significant popularity among Saudis. He was assassinated in 1975.

20- King Khalid: Khalid bin Abdul-Aziz Al Saud (Arabic: خَالد بن عبد العزيز آل سعود Khālid ibn 'Abd al-'Azīz Āl Su'ūd) (February 13, 1913–June 13, 1982) was King of Saudi Arabia from 1975 to 1982. He ruled during Saudi Arabia's oil boom years. In 1979, he had to deal with the Grand Mosque Seizure. As King, he delegated many of his responsibilities to his half-brother Crown Prince Fahd.

21- King Saud: Saud bin Abdul-Aziz Al Saud (January 12, 1902– February 23, 1969) (Arabic: سعود بن عبد العزيز آل سعود Su'ūd ibn 'Abd al-'Azīz Āl Su'ūd) was King of Saudi Arabia from 1953 to 1964. He handed the thrown to his brother Faisal after he fell ill. He was the eldest surviving son of Ibn Saud and became Crown Prince in 1933. He was known for courage and generosity. He died in Greece.

22- Madinah: Medina (English pronunciation: /mɛ di nə/; Arabic: المدينة المنورة, al-Madīnah al-Munawwarah, "the radiant city" [officially], or المدينة al-Madīnah; also transliterated as Madinah, or madinat al-nabi "the city of the prophet") is a city in the Hejaz region of western Saudi Arabia, and serves as the capital of the Al Madinah Province. It is the second holiest city in Islam, and the burial place of the Islamic Prophet Muhammad, and it is historically significant for being his home after the Hijrah. Before the advent of Islam, the city was known as Yathrib but was personally renamed by Muhammad. Medina is home to the three oldest mosques in Islam, namely Al-Masjid al-Nabawi (The Prophet's Mosque), Quba Mosque (the first mosque in Islam's history), and Masjid al-Qiblatain (the mosque where the qibla was switched to Mecca). Because of the Saudi government's religious policy and concern that historic sites could become the focus for idolatry, much of Medina's Islamic physical heritage has been destroyed since the beginning of

Saudi rule. The Islamic calendar is based on the emigration of Muhammad and his followers to the city of Medina, which marks the start of the Hijri year in 622 CE, called Hijra (هجرة). Similarly to Mecca, entrance to Medina is restricted to Muslims only; non-Muslims are neither permitted to enter nor travel through the city. Muslims believe that the latter verses of the Quran were revealed in Medina and its surrounding outskirts, called the medinan suras

23- Makkah: Mecca (/☐mɛkə/; Arabic: مكة, Makkah, pronounced [☐mæk☐ɐ]) is a city in the Hejaz and the capital of Makkah province in Saudi Arabia. The city is located 73 km (45 mi) inland from Jeddah in a narrow valley at a height of 277 m (909 ft) above sea level. Its resident population in 2008 was 1.7 million, although visitors more than double this number every year during Hajj period held in the twelfth Muslim lunar month of Dhu al-Hijjah. As the birthplace of Muhammad and a site of the composition of the Quran, Mecca is regarded as the holiest city in the religion of Islam, and a pilgrimage to it known as the Hajj is obligatory upon all able Muslims. The Hijaz was long ruled by Muhammad's descendants, the sharifs, either as independent rulers or as vassals to larger empires. It was absorbed into Saudi Arabia in 1925. In its modern period, Mecca has seen tremendous expansion in size and infrastructure. Because of this, Mecca has lost many thousand-years-old buildings and archaeological sites. Today, more than thirteen million Muslims visit Mecca annually, including several million during the few days of the Hajj. As a result, Mecca has become one of the most cosmopolitan and diverse cities in the Muslim world, although non-Muslims remain prohibited from entering the city.

24- Tazeer: In Islamic Law ta'zir, (Arabic تعزير) refers to punishment, usually corporal, that can be administered at the discretion of the judge, called a Qadi, Kadi (Judge), as opposed to the Hudod.

25- Qisas: Qisas (Arabic: قصاص) is an Islamic term meaning "Equal Retaliation," and follows the principle of an eye for an eye, or lex talionis, first set forth by Hammurabi. In the case of murder, it means the right of the heirs of a murder victim to demand execution of the murderer. The Qur'an also allows aggrieved parties to forfeit the right of qisas as an act of charity or in atonement for sins.

26- Quran: The Quran (English pronunciation: /kɒ□rɑ□n/ kor-AHN; Arabic: القرآن al-qur□ān, IPA: [qur□a□n],[variations] literally meaning "the recitation"), also transliterated Qur'an, Koran, Al-Coran, Qur'ān, Coran, Kuran, and Al-Qur'ān, is the central religious text of Islam, which Muslims consider the verbatim word of God (Arabic: الله, Allah). It is regarded widely as the finest piece of literature in the Arabic language

27- Rahma: Rahma means mercy. One of the names of God is Al-Rahman—the Most Merciful.

28- Ridda: Defined in Islam as the rejection in word or deed of one's former religion (apostasy) by a person who was previously a follower of Islam.

29- Sarika: Theft (Sarika, السرقة)

30- Shafa'a: The act of interceding (intervening or mediating) between two parties.

31- Shubha: Doubt, or uncertainty.

32- Shubuhat: The plural of the word shubha

33- Sitr: To conceal and veil.

34- Sunnah: The word Sunnah (سنة [□sunna], plural سنن sunan [□sunan], Arabic) literally means a clear, well-trodden, busy, and plain surfaced road. In the discussion of the sources of religion, Sunnah denotes the practice of Prophet Muhammad that he taught and practically instituted as a teacher of the sharī'ah and the best exemplar.

35- Wali Aldam: Closest blood relative.

36- Yemen: A region located in the southwestern to southern end of the Arabian Peninsula.

37- Zakat: One of the Five Pillars of Islam, zakat is the giving of a fixed portion of one's wealth to charity, generally to the poor and needy.

38- Zina: Zinā or Zinā□ (Arabic: الزنا) is generally defined by Islamic Law as unlawful sexual intercourse, i.e. intercourse between a man and a woman who are not married

39- Qathf: False accusation of Zina (Slander)

www.ingramcontent.com/pod-product-compliance
Lightning Source LLC
Chambersburg PA
CBHW022126170526
45157CB00004B/1771